ADVERTISEMENT.

THE following Essay is based on an article prepared for the Newport Advertiser, of whose columns the author of these sheets has, during the last six years, occasionally availed himself, for the examination of subjects of general interest. The original publication appeared, on the 16th of June, when it was supposed that we were on the eve of a protracted discussion with England, in reference to the visitation and search of our vessels, in time of peace. That matter, so far as regards the United States, is now understood to have been definitively settled by the acceptance, on the part of Great Britain, of the exposition of international law presented by the American Secretary of State, which, it was admitted, accorded with the judicial decisions of Lord Stowell, and with the parliamentary declarations of the Duke of Wellington. These views have since also received the sanction of the learned Ex-Chancellor, Lord Lyndhurst.

It is believed that the history of negotiations, involving the cardinal principles of maritime jurisprudence, cannot be without interest to the citizens of a nation having the largest navigation of any people; while the recognition of the independence of our flag may well absolve us from the onerous obligations assumed by the Ashburton Treaty, the objections to which were so fully pointed out, in the Senate, by our present chief magistrate, at the time of its ratification.

Aware that any claim which this work can have to notice must arise from the intrinsic accuracy of its views, the author has endeavored to apply, without either national or partisan prejudice, to facts, as they have arisen, the universally recognized rules of public law and political science. The statutory provisions of Great Britain speak for themselves. He trusts that no one will impute to him, because he has deemed it his duty to dissent from the course of Mr. Webster, on a matter connected with our foreign relations, any disrespect for the memory of one, who, by jeoparding for the Union an unequalled sectional popularity, added to the title of jurist and statesman that of patriot.

OCHRE POINT, NEWPORT, August 25, 1858.

CONTENTS.

VISITATION AND SEARCH.

VISITATION AND SEARCH.

THE people of the United States, averse to the maintenance of large military establishments, whether on the ocean or on the land, and having a commercial marine, which, never inconsiderable, is now the largest in the world, have always been deeply sensible of the vital importance of sustaining unimpaired their maritime rights. Of the truth of this assertion we have ample evidence in the unanimity which, regardless of all domestic differences, Congress manifested in reference to the late aggressions on our commerce in the Gulf of Mexico. Even sectional jealousies, and those anti-slavery sentiments which have so often menaced the existence of the Union, did not cause the ostensible object of British interference to stifle the patriotic denunciations, which a disregard to the immunity of our flag called forth from every part of the senate-house.

Coming into existence as a nation, when the States of continental Europe were arraying themselves against the inordinate pretensions of England, whose naval successes already augured such superiority as might jeopard the enjoyment, by the vessels of other countries, of the ocean as the common territory of all nations, the Congress of the Revolution promptly acceded to that declaration which has given immortality to Catharine of Russia. Our contemporaneous treaties embody stipulations for the immunity of the flag, which originated with or obtained the sanction of Franklin and Jefferson. Though our judiciary has recognized, as evidence of the law of nations, the decisions, which bound us, as at one time constituting a portion of the British empire, it has felt itself under no obligation to receive as law those interpolations into admiralty jurisprudence which had no other basis than acts of parliament or orders of the king in council, and which, at this day, are repudiated by even English publicists. Our diplomacy, which, in the early days of the republic, was confided to the first men of the nation, has been untiring in sustaining our rights as neutrals, in which relation, except during the war of 1812, we have, since the acknowledgment of our independence, ever stood towards the powers of Europe.

Indeed, it was outrages on our commerce that induced the quasi war with France in 1798; and similar causes, aggravated by the impressment of American seamen, brought on the war, which, comparatively feeble as we were, we honorably waged forty-six years ago against the mistress of the ocean. For other maritime spoliations, including subsequent injuries from imperial France, we received indemnities even less important as pecuniary compensations to individuals, than as acknowledgments due to our national honor. What we would not tolerate, when our population did not exceed one quarter of the present number, we will hardly pass by unnoticed, when our country has as many inhabitants as some of the most powerful empires, and our resources in other respects have more than proportionably increased. The recent offences are the less tolerable from having occurred in the Gulf of Mexico. If it be possible for any power to claim peculiar rights there, as England was wont to do in the seas adjacent to the British isles, it would be the United States.

The general pacification of Europe leaving us opposed, single-handed, to England, rendered it difficult, in 1814, to insist on the renunciation of the claim of impressment, while experience has shown that the attempt, in 1842, permanently to waive between two nations, having ships in every sea, a question that may recur whenever a British cruiser meets an American merchantman, is wholly impracticable. The losses to which the commercial world is constantly subjected by monetary panics, growing out of the fear of hostilities, whenever the British government chooses to issue new instructions to its cruisers, or they fall into the hands of officers disposed to obey them literally, render it a matter of primary importance that there should be no more temporary adjustments. And it happily appears that the British people are not now disposed, either for the purpose of accomplishing the abolition of the slave-trade, already rendered, by the substitution of nominal apprentices or "emigrants" to declared slaves, of little practical consequence to Africa, or even of maintaining, for their own political aggrandizement, a maritime police over the ocean, to encounter the risk of an interruption of intercourse with the nation on which they are dependent for the material of their most extended manufacture, and for which, since the revolt in India, even a partial substitute cannot be found.

The United States have always been more successful in negotiating with the party now in power than with those who have pretended to greater liberality in their political creed; and we do not deem it unfortunate that this question has been brought to a practical discussion in the ministry of the Earl of Derby, instead of that presided over by Lord Palmerston. Nor can the relations of England to France, as well as regards European politics as the particular subject of the African emigration, be otherwise than favorable to an adjustment of all difficulties between us and Great Britain.

Publicists consider the vessels of a nation on the high seas a portion of its territory. This, of course, excludes all maritime police and all jurisdiction over them on the part of any foreign State, and, so far as regards public ships, the rule admits of no exception. But, in time of war, what is usually denominated a right of visitation and search (*droit de visite* or *droit de visite et de recherche*) of merchant vessels, at least so far as may be necessary to verify their nationality and neutrality, is conceded to the lawfully commissioned cruisers of a belligerent, as essential to the exercise of the right of capturing enemy's ships, contraband of war, and vessels committing a breach of blockade. England has also contended, when no treaty intervenes, for a right of taking enemy's goods in neutral vessels. In cases, therefore, where the rule "free ships free goods" does not apply, a proportionate extension must be given to the claim in question. In the late war with Russia, Great Britain united with France in conceding immunity to enemy's property under such circumstances, while the latter power recognized her rule of considering neutral property on board of enemy's ships as free from capture. Other concessions were also introduced, which, were it not that Russia, against whom the war was waged, had no colonial trade to which the rule of '56 could be applicable, and few merchantmen to be affected, by the issue of letters of marque and reprisal to privateers, might have indicated an advance in civilization.

The modification of extreme belligerent rights was announced as only applying to the actual war, but it was subsequently adopted in a declaration made, at the congress of Paris, in April, 1856, by the plenipotentaries of Great Britain, Austria, France, Prussia, Russia, Sardinia, and Turkey. By that act, besides the two provisions, that the neutral flag covers enemy's goods with the exception of contraband of war, and that neutral goods, with the like exception, are not liable to capture under the enemy's flag, to which the treaties with Russia, Mexico, and Naples, concluded by us during the war, had been confined, it was declared that "blockades, in order to be binding, must be effective; that is to say, maintained by a force sufficient really to prevent access to the coast of the enemy," and that "privateering is and remains abolished."

The parties to the "declaration" engaged to bring it to the knowledge of the States that had not taken part in the congress of Paris, and invite their accession; and it was not to be deemed binding except between those which acceded to it. It was agreed by the plenipotentiaries, and inserted in the protocol of their proceedings, though not in the instrument itself, that the "declaration" was indivisible, and that the powers which signed it or should accede to it could not thereafter enter into any arrangement in regard to the application of the maritime law in time of war, which did not rest on the four principles which are the object of the "declaration." This provision it was, on the motion of the

Russian plenipotentiaries, admitted could not have any retroactive operation or invalidate any existing conventions, as it had also been conceded, at the suggestion of Count Orloff, that it would not be obligatory on the signers of the "declaration" to maintain the principle of the abolition of privateering against those powers which did not accede to it.

The whole propositions have, it is understood, received the sanction of most of the secondary powers of Europe and America. The definition as to blockade being in accordance with the rule of international law as always recognized by us, was not open to objection; but as the abolition of privateering, to which the United States can never assent while private property remains subject to capture by public ships, was one of them, the law of nations, as heretofore understood, must in any future war apply to us, except as regards those nations with which we had modified it by previous treaties.

However liberal the propositions of the congress may appear on their face, an examination of the protocols will show, that, while England was apparently making concessions to neutrals, the same policy, directed to universal maritime dominion, which, as will be seen, under the guise of humanity, has ever governed her course, in regard to the slave-trade, was her rule of conduct. At the conference at which they were adopted, "the Earl of Clarendon reminded the congress that England, as well as France, at the commencement of the war, had sought to mitigate its effects, and for that purpose had renounced in favor of neutrals, during the recent contest, principles which she had till then invariably maintained. He added, that England was disposed to renounce them definitively, provided that privateering is equally abolished for ever; that privateering is nothing else than an organized and legalized piracy; that privateers are the greatest scourges of war; and that our state of civilization and humanity requires that an end should be put to a system which does not belong to our age. If the whole congress assented to Count Walewski's proposition, it should be well understood that it would not be obligatory, except with regard to those powers which should accede to it, and that it could not be invoked by the governments which should refuse to adopt it."[1]

The great maritime States of the world are the United States, England, and France. The former, while she has the largest mercantile marine, possesses no navy bearing any proportion to those of the other two powers. The obvious result of the adoption of the naked proposition as to privateering, attempted to be introduced into the international code, without any consultation with us, would be (unless the rule was evaded by converting our merchantmen into public ships of war), in the event of a contest with either England or France, to drive our vessels from the ocean or subject them to the capture of the enemy's ships of war, while the merchantmen of the other belligerent would only be exposed to the comparatively few public cruisers of the United States. When the abolition of privateering was discussed, at the period of the recognition of our independence, by the statesmen and philosophers who then represented our diplomacy in Europe, and when it was proposed to be included in the negotiations of 1823–4 with England, it was always connected with the immunity of private property on the ocean. Indeed, the views of Franklin, Jefferson,

---

[1] Annuaire des Deux Mondes, 1855–6, p. 939.

and Adams, as incorporated in the treaty of 1785 with Prussia, went much further, and provided against any interference with industrial pursuits either at sea or on land.[1]

Nor was the British plenipotentiary, in associating, as it were, all the States of Europe in the adoption of a principle, which it was supposed would place the United States in a false position as regards the other powers of Christendom, unapprized of the insuperable objection to the adoption by them of the "Paris declaration," in the form in which it was presented. It had already been announced in one of the annual messages of President Pierce.[2] And even when, in March, 1854, in advance of the declaration of war, the suggestion was made as to the abolition of privateering by Lord Clarendon to Mr. Buchanan, our minister replied that "it did not seem to him possible, under existing circumstances, for the United States to agree to the suppression of privateering, unless the naval powers of the world would go one step further, and consent that war against private property should be abolished altogether upon the ocean, as it had already been upon the land. There was nothing really different in principle or morality between the act of a regular cruiser and that of a privateer in robbing a merchant vessel upon the ocean, and confiscating the property of private individuals on board for the benefit of the captor. Suppose a war with Great Britain: the navy of Great Britain was vastly superior to that of the United States in the number of vessels of war. The only means which we would possess to counterbalance, in some degree, their far

---

[1] U. S. Stat. at Large, Vol. VIII. p. 96.

[2] Cong. Doc., President's Message, December, 1854.

greater numerical strength, would be to convert our merchant vessels, cast out of employment by the war, into privateers, and endeavor, by their assistance, to inflict as much injury on the British as they would be able to inflict on American commerce."[1]

In the debate in the House of Lords, May 22, 1856, the Earl of Clarendon, in answer to the attack on him for having yielded the principle that "free ships make free goods," defended his course mainly on the ground that the "declaration" must be adopted as an entirety or not at all, and that, if the United States accepted it, they must acquiesce in the abandonment of privateering, which was to England more than an equivalent for a claim (taking enemy's property in neutral vessels) that she could not maintain; that privateering must become more important than heretofore, as commerce carried on in sailing ships would be absolutely at the mercy of a privateer moved by steam, however small. The Earl of Harrowby, in sustaining the ministry, said that England had suffered more injury from privateering than she could inflict, and that the United States would derive no benefit from the treaty, if they did not agree to abandon it.

On the other hand, it is not uninteresting to notice that the opponents of the then ministry, while earnestly contending against immunity to enemy's goods as calculated, as between France and England, to operate altogether to the benefit of the former, also urged the consequences of the adoption of the "declaration," as affecting the relations of the latter with the United States. The Earl of Hardwicke said: "France would man her navy

---

[1] Cong. Doc. 33 Cong. 1 S. H. R. Ex. Doc. No. 103.

from her merchantmen, looking to neutral carriers, while, as America never would abandon the right of privateering, the course we are now taking would give direct offence to one of the greatest commercial nations of the world." The Earl of Derby admitted that there were very weighty reasons in the late war, when France and England were allies, for waiving the exercise of the right of taking enemy's goods under neutral flags, but that to give it up permanently was an abandonment of British naval superiority. Under the rule, as previously contended for by England, "in case of war against France, you could prevent her sending a single bale of cotton to sea. Now, she will make her merchantmen vessels of war, and have seamen for them, by sending away every thing under neutral flags. And, as there is the highest authority for believing that America will not give up privateering, you direct your threats exclusively at her, because you say that the limited advantages which are given to neutrals shall only be shared by those who adhere to this declaration as an entirety. You make the hostility of America more pointed by maintaining against her the right of search, whilst the maritime law is relaxed as to others." [1]

The American government, it is well known, offered, through Mr. Marcy, to accept the whole "declaration," in case the clause abolishing privateering should be amended, by adding "that the private property of the subjects or citizens of a belligerent on the high seas shall be exempted from seizure by public armed vessels of the other belligerent, except it be contraband."

The counter proposition was sustained in a most able

---

[1] Hansard's Parl. Deb. N. S. Vol. CXLII. p. 482.

note from the American Secretary of State to the Count de Sartiges, under date of July 28, 1856.[1] It has, however, been made a question, whether even such an arrangement as was proposed by us would not have subjected the United States to disproportionate sacrifices. We neither maintain large standing armies nor permanent navies. On land we resort to volunteers, and we have been in the habit of regarding our privateersmen as the "militia of the ocean." In a document emanating from the present House of Representatives, it is said that there were fifteen thousand men employed in the private armed service during the last war with England. "That war," it is added, "was brought to a speedy close by the pressure of public sentiment prevailing throughout Great Britain. The occasion of this sentiment was that American privateers were rapidly destroying her commerce, and affecting, directly and indirectly, every branch of business enterprise." [2]

At all events, it is to be hoped, that, if our government should enter into further negotiations on this subject, no convention will be concluded that will not reach the whole evil arising from a claim of the right of search, and that the entire immunity of the neutral flag, beyond ascertaining its nationality, will be established. The admission that the flag covers enemy's goods would effect that object, were it not for the exception of contraband of war. Nor does there appear to be any advantage to the belligerent, in the continuance of the rule of contraband, commensurate with the injuries which it must inevitably cause to the neutral in the

---

[1] Cong. Doc., Pres. Message, Aug. 12, 1856.

[2] Report of the Committee on Naval Affairs, May 4, 1858.

detention of his ships and the interruption of his trade, and from the collisions between neutrals and belligerents, to which the exercise of the right of search must give rise. As destination to an enemy's port is an essential point in a question of contraband, in all cases where the rule is of any practical importance to a belligerent, the law of blockade also intervenes.[1]

This matter seems to have been fully appreciated by those who opposed, in parliament, the new maritime code. Lord Colchester said, "contraband of war was expressly excepted from the arrangement, and how could belligerents know whether a neutral vessel had contraband on board, without stopping and searching her?" The Earl of Derby remarked, "You maintain the principle that neutrals may be searched for contraband of war, and you thereby admit the principle of the violation of the neutral flag, and you continue the danger and inconvenience which result to merchantmen from being overhauled at sea. If you grant one principle you must grant another, and give entire immunity to private property." [2]

Abolish contraband, and we should remove from the belligerents all excuse for violating that nationality which, in war as well as in peace, should attach to every ship as a portion of the country to which it belongs. Such an arrangement would prevent forever an abuse, against which the negotiations of seventy years have been unable to provide, and which, notwithstanding the able argument presented by Mr. Webster to Lord Ashburton, is still as open to discussion as ever.

---

[1] Wheaton's Elements, Lawrence's Ed. p. 572, note.

[2] Hansard's Debates, ut supra, p. 522.

It will be remembered that it was never claimed that the officer of a British man-of-war could enter a neutral vessel for the purpose of searching for seamen. In the declaration of the Prince Regent in January, 1813, in reference to the causes of the American war, it is said: "His Royal Highness can never admit, that, in the exercise of the undoubted and hitherto undisputed right of searching neutral merchant vessels in time of war, the impressment of British seamen, when found therein, can be deemed any violation of a neutral flag. Neither can he admit that the taking such seamen from on board such vessels can be considered by any neutral State as a hostile measure, or a justifiable cause of war." This document, originating from the highest source, is here quoted, not only for the purpose of showing that with the extinction of the right of search the apology for impressment would cease, but in order to keep in view the nature of those British pretensions against which it becomes us incessantly to guard.

We will not discuss the doctrine of indefeasible allegiance, which England herself would seem, from her liberal Naturalization Act of 1844, no longer to regard as essential, but our view of British pretensions and of British morals might be imperfect, without the citation of a paragraph from this extraordinary State paper, showing that native born Americans were confessedly included, as unfortunately was but too well authenticated, in the comprehensive system of man-stealing sanctioned by royal authority.

"If a similarity of language and manners," says the Prince Regent, "may make the exercise of this right more liable to partial mistakes, and occasional abuse, when practised towards vessels of the United States, the same circumstances make it also a right, with the exercise of which, in regard to such vessels, it is more difficult to dispense."[1]

The disregard of our sovereignty by entering, as it were, into our territory, and kidnapping our citizens, at the caprice of any British midshipman, not to make them merely ordinary slaves, but to expose their lives in fighting for those who had no claim on their allegiance, and in some cases against their own country (for there were many impressed American seamen in the British navy during the war of 1812), is thus made more flagrant by the bold avowal of a fraudulent perversion of a neutral concession.

It may also be noticed in this connection, that, as in the analogous case of the search for slavers, the intolerable inconveniences arising from its unauthorized exercise were used to extort the admission of a search for seamen under mitigated circumstances. The proposition for a modified right is alluded to in the following instructions of Mr. Secretary Monroe to the plenipotentiaries at Ghent. "It has been suggested as an expedient mode, for the adjustment of this controversy, that British cruisers should have a right to search our vessels for British seamen; but that the commanders thereof should be subjected to penalties in case they made mistakes and took from them American citizens. By this the British government would acquire the right of search for seamen, with that of impressing from our vessels the subjects of all other powers. It will not escape your attention, that, by admitting the right, in any case, we give up the principle, and leave the door open to every kind of abuse. The same objection is applicable to any, and

---

[1] Annual Register, 1813, p. 339.

every other arrangement, which withholds the respect due to our flag, by not allowing it to protect the crew sailing under it."[1]

With the illustration before us of the abuses of which the exercise of the assumed right of search is susceptible, it might well become all nations that regard their independence to inquire with Hautefeuille whether, even as a belligerent right, it can be sustained at all, on principle. That most able expounder of the rights and duties of neutrals, who does not confine his investigation to the practice of nations nor to the opinions of previous institutional writers, is unwilling to extend the *droit de visite* beyond a verification of the nationality of the ship, and, when bound to an enemy's port, the nature of the cargo, with reference to contraband, including (in the case of those who reject, contrary to what he deems the correct rule, the principle that the flag covers the merchandise) the nationality of the cargo. He distinguishes between *visite,* which by other French commentators is deemed equivalent to the English *visitation and search,* and *recherche* (search), which he treats under a distinct head. The former he considers a belligerent right, and the latter the exercise of a jurisdictional act of sovereignty. As all the pretence which a belligerent can have to interfere with the unrestricted use of the ocean by neutrals arises from considerations of self-defence, of the right to prevent acts which, in their result, may enure to the benefit of the enemy, he contends that this is satisfied when the regularity of the papers relating to the ship and cargo is ascertained. He denies the right of making inquisitorial searches by opening the hatchways,

---

[1] Wait's American State Papers, Vol. IX. p. 344.

and interrogating the crew with a view of discrediting the official papers. Much less does he admit of the seizure on suspicion of the vessel, and treating it as an enemy's ship, till the tribunal of the belligerent shall otherwise decide.[1]

But whatever may be the law of nations as to the extent of the conflicting rights of belligerents and neutrals, no ground on which it has been attempted to justify the detention of merchant vessels by ships of war, at sea, is applicable to a time of peace. It may be unhesitatingly asserted as an historical fact, that, before the general pacification of Europe, in 1814–15, not only was no claim of this nature ever made as of right but it had never been asked to be conceded by one power to another as a matter of conventional arrangement. Visitation and search in peace, by the public ships of one country of the merchant vessels of another, originated with Great Britain, and grew out of a policy which was intended to perpetuate that maritime police which her great navy had, except when occasionally thwarted by American enterprise and bravery, exclusively exercised over the ocean during the long wars growing out of the first French Revolution.

At the congress of Vienna, circumstances were peculiarly favorable to England. In the contest in which the States of Europe had just been embarked, it was against the country of Napoleon, who had absorbed their territories within his mighty empire or held them annexed as dependent principalities, that their jealousy was directed. They had no apprehensions of England, no widely extended commerce to be affected by that mari-

---

[1] Hautefeuille. — Droits des Nations Neutres, tit. xi. xii.

time superiority, which had, indeed, enabled her to supply the very largesses which had so essentially contributed to the success of the coalition. The United States, of course, had no part in those proceedings, and it might well have been supposed that France, the only European State that could have contemplated a maritime rivalry with England, was, as a conquered country, in no position to counteract British influence. It was, moreover, the good fortune of England to be able to mask her ambition under the guise of humanity. From being not only the importer of African slaves to her own colonial possessions, but the privileged carrier for other nations, she suddenly learned that the traffic was a violation of justice and humanity, and, like all new converts, she had no commiseration for those who did not at once adopt her views, and repudiate the opinions, which, however erroneous, from the time of the virtuous Las Casas, had been entertained alike by ecclesiastics and statesmen.

Already, while the wars were still waging, had England applied to the ships of other countries her newly adopted principles in relation to the slave-trade. In 1807, the American ship Amadie,[1] employed in carrying slaves from the coast of Africa to a Spanish colony, was condemned by the Lords of Appeals in prize causes, because, the British legislature having abolished the slave-trade as contrary to the principles of justice and humanity, it was incumbent on the claimant to show that it was authorized by the laws of his own country. And, in conformity with this precedent, Lord Stowell in 1811 condemned another American vessel, The Fortuna,[2]

[1] Acton's Admiralty Reports, Vol. I. p. 240.

[2] Dodson's Admiralty Reports, Vol. I. p. 81.

while he restored to the Swedish owner The Diana,[1] on the ground that Sweden had not then prohibited the trade by law or convention, and still continued to tolerate it in practice.

It is difficult to sustain the foregoing condemnations on any recognized principle. The reasoning of the courts is somewhat of the same character with the Prince Regent's argument, justifying the perversion of a belligerent right to the enforcement of a municipal law for a purpose for which it was never conceded. These vessels were entered and seized on the belligerent claim of visitation and search, and were thus brought within the jurisdiction of a prize court, while their neutrality, the only legitimate matter of inquiry, was recognized in a way confessedly to entitle the owners to restitution. The judge, assuming the office of a general *custos morum*, decided, that, because it had not been affirmatively proved that they were engaged in a trade authorized by the laws of the United States, they should be condemned. Whether the views of Sir William Grant, who pronounced the opinion of the Court of Appeals, were in anywise influenced by the fact that the neutral claimants were Americans, might be a matter of curious speculation. It may be remarked, that the decrees of condemnation were rendered contemporaneously with those numerous edicts, known as Orders in Council, issued against our commerce, which the courts, as well as institutional writers of England, now admit to have been repugnant to international law.

There was no delay on the part of England in her efforts to inaugurate her system of a perpetual maritime

---

[1] Dodson's Admiralty Reports, Vol. I. p. 95.

police. The Treaty of Paris, by one of the separate articles of which France engaged to unite her efforts with Great Britain, at a future congress, to cause all the powers of Christendom to proclaim the abolition of the slave-trade, was signed on the 30th of May, 1814. On the 6th of August, in advance of the congress of Vienna, Lord Castlereagh instructed the Duke of Wellington, then ambassador to Paris, that "a second regulation, highly important to prevail on France to accede to, is, a reciprocal permission to our respective cruisers, within certain latitudes, to visit the merchant ships of the other powers, and if found with slaves on board, in contravention of the law of their particular state, to carry or send them in for adjudication." The Duke of Wellington accordingly addressed the Prince of Benevento (Talleyrand) on the subject; but he writes, on the 5th of November, in reference to the proposition, "that it was so disagreeable to the government, and that (he) had seen in different publications that it was likely to be so much so to the nation, that there was no chance of succeeding in getting it adopted."

Nor was England more fortunate in her attempt to obtain the coöperation of Portugal, so long her dependent ally. As we learn from a protocol of a special conference at Vienna on the 28th of January, 1815, Lord Castlereagh having suggested, as the surest mode of putting an end to the traffic, the *exercise* of a *police* against those vessels that should engage in the trade, Prince Talleyrand asked the British plenipotentiary to define the meaning of the term. Lord Castlereagh assured him that he meant such a *police* as every government exercised by virtue of its own sovereignty, or of special treaties with other powers. Thereupon Prince

Talleyrand and the Count Palmella (Portuguese Minister) said that they did not recognize the exercise of any maritime police, except that which each power exercises for itself, over its own vessels (*qu'ils n'admettoient en fait de police maritime que celle que chaque puissance excerce sur ses propres bâtimens*).

Another project was brought forward at Vienna with as little success. England endeavored to make the abolition of the slave-trade as subservient to her material interests as the maritime police would have been to her political power. She proposed the prohibition of the importation, into the dominions of the powers represented in the congress, of colonial produce, the growth of any colony where the slave-trade should still continue to be tolerated, and that they should only admit the productions of the colonies where the trade was unlawful, and of "those vast regions of the globe furnishing the same productions by the labor of their own inhabitants."[1] The British Indies were of course here referred to. How far Lord Castlereagh was justified in declaring of them, by way of contrast to countries cultivated by African labor, that their interests conformed to the "principles of humanity and religion," may be best determined by the fact that a cardinal principle of the English policy in India has ever been to interdict the propagation of the Christian religion, and that the conquerors and conquered are now vying with each other in the infliction of barbarities, scarcely known to history since the Spanish invasion of the American continent.

---

[1] Schoell — Histoire des Traités, tom. xi. p. 188.

The only general result of these negotiations was a declaration, bearing date 8th of February, 1815, of adherence by the congress to the additional article of the treaty of Paris between England and France, denouncing the trade as "*repugnant to the principles of humanity and of universal morality,*" but leaving the period for its abolition a subject of negotiation between the several powers.[1]

Two treaties were signed at Vienna between England and Portugal, but they cannot be considered as having materially advanced the ostensible cause, in which the former was so warmly enlisted, much less did they favor her scheme of a maritime police. On the contrary, one of them made provision for the ships of Portugal, which had been detained and condemned by Great Britain on the alleged ground of being engaged in an illicit traffic in slaves. The other, having special reference to the slave-trade and providing for its partial abolition, in consideration of the release of a debt due from Portugal, was scarcely in advance of the treaty of Rio de Janeiro of 1810, the first conventional arrangement entered into by England on that subject, and which was then annulled.[2]

The treaty of September, 1817, with Spain, and the operation of which was extended in 1822 and in 1835, inaugurated, though the trade was still partially allowed till 1820, the general system of reciprocal search, which had been yielded by Portugal the preceding July, as to the trade interdicted by her north of the equator. In

---

[1] Flassan — Histoire du Congrès de Vienne, tom. iii. p. 286.

[2] Martens — Recueil des Traités, S. tom. vi. pp. 93–96.

the discussions in parliament on the Spanish treaty, "the introduction of the right of search, and the bringing in for condemnation, in *time of peace,* was declared to be a *precedent* of the utmost importance." No one then contended for any such power, independent of treaty.

It was soon after the Spanish convention was concluded (Dec. 15, 1817), that Lord Stowell (Sir William Scott), without adverting to the previous adjudications, delivered his judgment in the case of the French vessel The Louis, captured 11th March, 1816, and condemned, at Sierra Leone, because the brig, being engaged in the slave-trade contrary to the laws of France and the law of nations, could derive no protection from the French, or any other flag, and because she had resisted the British cruiser, and *piratically* killed eight of her men, and had resisted *search.*

Lord Stowell decided that no British act of parliament, or commission founded on it, if inconsistent with the law of nations, can affect the rights or interests of foreigners, that the right of visitation and search on the high seas does not exist in peace, that trading in slaves is not piracy nor a *crime* by the universal law of nations. He says, referring to the declaration at the congress of Vienna, that, "great as the reverence due to such authorities may be, they cannot be admitted to have the force of overruling the established course of the general law of nations."

He decided further that a nation "has a right to see that its own vessels are duly navigated, but it has no right in consequence to visit and search all the apparent vessels of other countries on the high seas, in order to institute an inquiry whether they are not in truth British vessels violating British laws," — that the penalties imposed by a French law must be enforced, not in an English, but in a French, court.

He adds what, if not an authoritative portion of his opinion, coming from such a source as Lord Stowell, is entitled to no slight attention on the part of those who direct the international relations of England, while it renders clearer, if possible, his views as to the strictly belligerent character of a right of visitation and search. "If," says he, "I felt it necessary to press the consideration further, it would be by stating the gigantic mischiefs which such a claim is likely to produce. It is no secret, particularly in this place, that the right of search, in time of war, though unquestionable, is not submitted to without complaints broad and bitter, in spite of all the modifications that can be applied to it. If this right of war is imported into peace by convention, it will be for the prudence of states to regulate by that convention the exercise of the rights with all the softenings of which it is capable." After questioning whether it can even then be made tolerable, it being, as he said, "the exercise of a right which *pro tanto* converts a state of peace into a state of war," Lord Stowell proceeds: "But if it be assumed by force and left at large to operate reciprocally upon the ships of every state (for it must be a right of All against All) without any other limits as to time, place, or mode of inquiry, than such as the prudence of particular states or their individual subjects may impose, I leave the tragedy contained in this case to illustrate the effects that are likely to arise in the very first stages of the process, without adding to the account, what must be considered as a most awful part of it, the perpetual irritation and universal hostility which are likely to ensue." [1]

It does not detract from the force of Lord Stowell's argument, that he might, on the authority of The Diana, have decreed restitution, without deciding the great principle which he so fully discussed. He does, indeed, come to the conclusion, that, at the date of her capture, there was no French ordinance for abolishing the traffic, he not deeming the recital to that effect in the treaty of November 20, 1815, between England and France, to be sustained by the documents before him.

Nor was The Louis an isolated case of restitution to foreign owners of ships alleged to be engaged in the slave-trade. Several decrees were made by the Court of Admiralty in favor of Spaniards, in regard to vessels illegally captured and detained on account of their participation in that traffic, and the compensation for their indemnity is included in the £400,000 stipulated in the treaty of September, 1817, to be paid by England to Spain, as the price of her assent to the abolition of the trade.

The principles settled in The Louis were reaffirmed by Lord Stowell, in 1824, in the case of The San Juan Nepomuceno, captured in December, 1817, and consequently after the treaty, and condemned at Sierra Leone.[2]

The English government, which had, in July, 1816, announced by a circular to its naval commanders, that the right of search, being a belligerent right, had ceased with the war, again attempted in vain, in 1818, to procure its concession from France. In May of that year,

---

[1] Dodson's Admiralty Reports, Vol. II. p. 210.
[2] Haggard's Admiralty Reports, Vol. I. p. 267.

a treaty of that nature was concluded with the Netherlands,[1] and, at the congress of Aix la Chapelle, in November, the subject was brought anew to the consideration of the great powers; but Austria, Russia, and Prussia then refused either to allow the reciprocal right of search, applicable to all nations which had prohibited the slave-trade, or to proclaim the traffic piracy under the law of nations. As at Vienna, the congress confined itself to a general declaration respecting the odious character of the commerce.

Nor was more effected at Verona in 1822. The French government explicitly rejected both the propositions, — to make the trade piracy, and to allow a right of search. As to the latter point, Mr. Chateaubriand declared his government could never consent, and that any attempt to exercise it between the French and English would be attended with the most fatal consequences. Indeed, the government of the restoration seemed fully aware that the offer of reciprocity was entirely illusory, and that the system could only operate for the aggrandizement of England.

The Treaty of Ghent of 1814, by which peace was restored between the United States and Great Britain, and which pledged both parties to use their best endeavors for the abolition of the slave-trade, afforded to the latter an opportunity to bring us within the operation of her maritime police. To propositions, made to our government, a short time before the meeting at Aix la Chapelle, of the same character as those submitted to the congress, Mr. Adams, Secretary of State, under date of November 2, 1818, replied: "That the admission of

---

[1] Further treaties were made with the Netherlands in 1822, 1823, and 1837.

a right in the officers of foreign ships of war to enter and search the vessels of the United States, in time of peace, under any circumstances whatever, would meet with universal repugnance in the public opinion of the country."

Apart from the distrust, necessarily occasioned by the avowal of the Prince Regent, that a right of search, conceded for a legitimate purpose, might be perverted to any use that suited the interest of the party exercising it, it is impossible to conceive of a compact marked by grosser inequality, under the guise of reciprocity, unless it be the abolition of privateering, leaving private property, at sea, subject to capture by public ships, than a mutual right of search between two nations of equivalent mercantile tonnage, the one of which had only ten or a dozen cruisers, while the other possessed hundreds.

But the same popular abhorrence of the slave-trade, which elsewhere favored the British scheme of a maritime police, was scarcely less efficient in its behalf in the United States. Even those who were intrusted with the management of our public concerns seem to have forgotten the lessons which dear-bought experience had so recently taught them.

In January, 1818, and before any communication was made by Lord Castlereagh to Mr. Rush, the subject of a concert with foreign nations, in reference to the slave-trade, had been introduced into the Senate by Mr. Burrill of Rhode Island;[1] and the same year an act was passed rendering more stringent the laws against American citizens engaged in it. This, at the next session

[1] Benton's Abridged Debates, Vol. VI. p. 12.

of Congress, was followed by an act authorizing the President to employ our armed ships for the suppression of the trade, dividing the proceeds of slavers among the captors and giving a bounty of $25, for each negro.

The proposition for a coöperation with other powers, and involving a reciprocal right of search, occupied the attention of the House of Representatives at five successive sessions, commencing with 1820. By a law of May the 15th of that year the slave-trade was made piracy, and punishable, on conviction before a circuit court of the United States, by death.[1] The object of passing the act would seem to have been not to apply to an offence cognizable in our own courts only, a term applicable to a crime everywhere justiciable, and which might therefore give rise to constant mistakes; but it was adopted, on the expectation that the slave-trade would be made piracy by the law of nations, and thereby preclude all questions as to the right of search. Lord Stowell has adverted to the difficulty, if not impracticability, of obtaining such a sanction for it as would justify the insertion of a new crime into the international code. And all must be sensible of the inconvenience which he shows would result from enforcing such a provision, indiscriminately by all nations against the citizens of all nations. At all events, under existing circumstances, no satisfactory reason would seem to exist for preserving the misnomer, which, if not obnoxious to the graver objection of misleading naval officers, is apt to be regarded by the popular mind as an apology for the British pretensions.

---

[1] U S. Statutes at Large, Vol. V. p. 600.

Resolutions, founded on elaborate reports, in which an anxious desire to effect an object then paramount in the public mind, induced the House of Representatives to overlook the insuperable objections to a British maritime police, were passed in 1821, 1822, and 1823. The President was requested to enter into arrangements with other powers for the effectual abolition of the African slave-trade, and on the last occasion a clause was appended proposing its denunciation as piracy under the law of nations. The vote, in 1823, was nearly unanimous, though an amendment giving an *express* assent to a qualified right of search was rejected.

Under these circumstances, Mr. Rush was instructed to propose to England an arrangement which resulted in a convention, signed on 13th of March, 1824. This treaty, while it conceded a mutual right of search within certain limits, substituted for the mixed tribunals objected to by us as being inconsistent with our constitution, a provision that the captured vessels should be sent before the tribunals of their own country. England had been required, as a preliminary to any convention, to pass a statute, making, as we had done, the slave-trade piracy.[1]

When the convention was returned to the United States, the Senate ratified it with amendments, one of which struck out "America" from the assigned cruising grounds, which originally included the "coasts of Africa, of America, and of the West Indies." To this the British

---

[1] Cong. Doc. 18 Cong. 2 Sess. Doc. 2. The Earl of Harrowby said in the House of Lords, that, "unless the law passes, the convention cannot be carried into effect, but the bill and treaty are independent, and so they are in America. Whether the treaty is ratified or not, the slave-trade will be piracy by the laws of both countries."—Hansard's Parliamentary Debates, N. S. Vol. XI. p. 1.

secretary, Mr. Canning, would not assent; and to a subsequent proposal through Mr. Addington to conclude a new convention adopting the Senate's amendments, with the exception of the erasure of "America," Mr. Adams, on the 4th of December, 1824, replied, that the President had determined "to refer the whole subject to the deliberate advisement of Congress." This was done in the last annual message of Mr. Monroe. He there says: "As objections to the principle recommended by the House of Representatives, or at least to the consequences inseparable from it, and which are understood to apply to the law, have been raised, which may deserve a reconsideration of the whole subject, I have thought it proper to suspend the conclusion of a new convention until the definitive sentiments of congress may be ascertained." [1]

The Senate having subsequently rejected a similar treaty with Colombia, from which "the coasts of America" were excepted, Mr. Clay wrote to Mr. Addington, April 6, 1825, that "it would seem to be unnecessary and inexpedient any longer to continue the negotiation respecting the slave convention, with any hope that it can be made to assume a form satisfactory to both parties." [2]

Thus, through the obstinate adherence of Mr. Canning to a point which, as the principle was conceded by us, was of no significance, did we escape from an obligation, that, even if it had not led to the permanent establishment of a British police in our immediate neighborhood (for permission to cruise on the "coasts of the West Indies" would have included the Gulf of Mexico), could

---

[1] Annual Register, 1824, p. 119*.

[2] Annual Register, 1825, p. 61*.

scarcely have resulted otherwise than in continual collisions.[1]

In 1825, the subject of the slave-trade came before the Supreme Court of the United States, in the case of The Antelope. Marshall, Chief Justice, delivering the opinion of the court, held: "As no nation can prescribe a rule for others, none can make a law of nations; and the traffic remains lawful to those whose governments have not forbidden it.

"If it is consistent with the law of nations, it cannot in itself be piracy. It can be made so only by statute; and the obligations of the statute cannot transcend the legislative power of the State which may enact it.

"If it be neither repugnant to the law of nations, nor piracy, the right of bringing in for adjudication, in time of peace, even where the vessel belongs to a nation which has prohibited the trade, cannot exist. The courts of no country execute the penal laws of another; and the course of the American government on the subject of visitation and search would decide any case in which that right had been exercised by an American cruiser on the vessel of a foreign nation, not violating our municipal laws, against the captors."[2]

And in The Marianna Flora, decided in 1826, it was held, that the right of visitation and search, in peace, does not belong to the public ships of any nation. This right is strictly a belligerent right, allowed by the general consent of nations in time of war, and limited to those occasions. As to public ships, there is no reason why

---

[1] The mistake of Mr. Canning was alluded to, in 1843, in the discussion of the Ashburton Treaty, by Lord Brougham, who considered the American alteration proper, and by Sir Robert Peel. Annual Register, 1843, p. 14].

[2] Wheaton's Reports, Vol. X. p. 122.

they may not approach any vessels descried at sea for the purpose of ascertaining their real character; but, on the other hand, no ship is under such circumstances bound to lie by or wait the approach of any other ship.[1]

Before leaving this branch of our subject, we would refer to the French adjudications, which correspond with those of the English and American courts as to the absence of all jurisdiction over foreign vessels engaged in the slave-trade. Such was the decision of the *Commission des Prises* of Martinique of the 10th of April, 1824, in the case of an American vessel captured by a French frigate, and of the *Commission des Prises* of the Isle of Bourbon, 10th December, 1840, in the case of a Portuguese brig, captured both as a pirate and as a slaver. On the latter charge, the commission says, that, however culpable the acts of the captain and crew might have been, they are not punishable by the French tribunals, "because no convention between France and Portugal authorizes the capture of slave ships, and the punishment of their captains and crews."[2]

In 1824 a treaty was made with Sweden. And in 1826 one was concluded with Brazil, to which we may hereafter have occasion to refer, for the total abolition of the slave-trade in three years, after which it was to be deemed and treated as piracy. In the mean time, it was to be regulated in conformity with the provisions of the treaties of 1815 and of 1817 with Portugal.

The next important proceeding of England was the conclusion of the conventions of 1831 and 1833 with France, by which the right of search, so repeatedly solic-

---

[1] Wheaton's Reports, Vol. XI. p. 42.

[2] De Pistoye & Duverdy — Traité des Prises, tom. 1, p. 75.

ited since 1814, was acquired. Not only did the government of Louis Philippe make this concession, but it obtained the adhesion to the treaties, of Denmark and Sardinia in 1834, of the Hanse Towns and Tuscany in 1837, of Naples in 1838, and of Hayti in 1839.

The Duke de Broglie, who signed the conventions, some years afterwards defended them on the ground, that, during the whole reign of the elder Bourbons, and particularly from 1822 to 1830, French vessels, as well as American [of the latter he read a list of twenty], had actually been searched and seized by British cruisers, and finally condemned. "As when those conventions were made," he added, "all continental Europe was arrayed against France, she could not refuse to share with the only State that had manifested a sympathy in the revolution, a power which that State had exclusively exercised under the government of the restoration." [1]

In 1834 the abolition of slavery in the West Indies went into operation. Eight hundred thousand slaves were to be emancipated, for which Great Britain paid an indemnity to the West India proprietors of £20,000,000.

Whether impelled by the disastrous result of that experiment, or emboldened by the treaties which had been made to secure the right of search, and the impunity which had attended the violation of the flag of countries that had not entered into any conventional arrangements with her, England, in 1839, assumed to accomplish, by the authority of her own legislature, what could not be effected with the consent of other nations. An act (2 & 3 Vict. c. 73) was passed, which, although

---

[1] Annual Register, 1843, p. 276].

expressly aimed at Portugal, placed the mercantile marine of all nations at the mercy of the British navy, and is a parliamentary sanction for all the aggressions of which we have had to complain.

The offence of Portugal was not so much that she had not complied with her treaty stipulations, as that she would not enter into new engagements required by the policy or interests of England. Even if the treaties had been violated, the redress was by negotiation and not by parliamentary enactment, as was well remarked by the Duke of Wellington. Adverting to the fact that one of the clauses made it lawful to detain any vessels whatever, on suspicion, on the high seas, and demand their papers, and the persons exercising such authority were moreover indemnified from all consequences, he asked, "Was it intended that the vessels of any power in Europe might be searched and afterwards allowed to proceed on their voyage, whether we had treaties with those powers or not?" The answer of the Premier, Lord Melbourne, was little calculated to satisfy foreign States. "The bill," he said, "did not bind her to adopt those measures. It was for her Majesty to apportion her measures to meet the necessities of the case." The intention to interpolate the English municipal law into the law of nations was thus clearly admitted.

The act gave power to any person acting under the authority of the admiralty or of a secretary of state, not only to detain, for the purpose of examining the papers, but to seize and capture, the vessels of any nation whatever supposed to be connected with the slave-trade.[1] Jurisdiction is given to the courts of ad-

---

[1] The bill had passed the House of Commons with the following words in the second clause: "That in case her Majesty should please to issue orders

miralty over any Portuguese vessel or any vessel which shall not establish, to the satisfaction of such court, that she is justly entitled to claim the protection of the flag of a State or nation, and to condemn any such vessel and adjudge as to slaves found therein, in like manner and under such and the like rules and regulations as are contained in any act of parliament in force, in relation to the suppression of the slave-trade by British owned ships.[1]

It also condemned vessels on account of their suspicious equipments, unless it was shown that they were intended for a legal trade. The same bounties as in the case of the capture of British ships were also given to the captors, as well for the vessel as for the slaves, and the treasury was authorized to pay a portion of them in case of the death of a slave before condemnation. The slaves were also to be disposed of, as if taken in British ships.[2] And by a further Act of 5 & 6 Vict. (1842) c. 91, the net proceeds of the foreign vessels condemned were to be paid to the captors.[3]

---

to her cruisers to capture Portuguese vessels engaged in the slave-trade, or *vessels engaged in the slave-trade, not having on board, or the masters whereof should neglect to produce on demand, papers showing to the subjects of what State such vessels belong."* This was amended, on motion of Lord Lyndhurst, in the House of Lords, by substituting for the words in italic, "or any other vessels engaged in the slave-trade and not *justly* entitled to claim the protection of any flag." Practically the change of phraseology is unimportant; but the original draft still more clearly discloses the intent of the bill as to the exercise of the claim of *search.*

[1] It was decided, on appeal, in the case of the Portuguese ship The Thirteenth of June, condemned under this act, that the seizure, which was made at Rio de Janeiro, was for a violation of the municipal laws of Great Britain, and that, therefore, the proceedings were properly according to the provisions of the statute against British ships, and not according to the forms of the civil law. — (4 Moore's Privy Council Reports, p. 184.)

[2] British St. at Large, Vol. LXXIX. p. 441.

[3] Ib. vol. LXXXII. c. 782.

No one, on a question of this nature, could have been entitled to more consideration than the Duke of Wellington. As a plenipotentiary at Paris and at Vienna, and subsequently at Aix la Chapelle and at Verona, on all which occasions the right of search, in peace, was deliberately considered in reference to the slave-trade, he well understood that it could only exist as a voluntary concession. His opposition to the measure was rendered in every appropriate mode which parliamentary usage justified. Nor did he refrain, in referring to its possible application to us, from declaring, that, "if there was one point more to be avoided than another, it was that relating to the visitation of vessels belonging to the United States." "Nothing went to show the least disposition, on their part, to permit the right of detention and search for papers." And he added, after a protest against the third reading, "The measure still exhibited its criminal character. It was a breach of the law of nations, — a violation of international treaties, — and would go much further to encourage than to prevent the traffic against which its enactments were directed."[1]

Lord Stowell had, in the memorable judgment in the case of The Louis, among the positions which we have already quoted, laid it down, that "neither a British act of parliament, nor any commission founded on it, can affect any right or interest of foreigners unless they are founded upon principles and impose regulations that are consistent with the law of nations;"[2] but the authority of the first admiralty judge that England ever possessed was no more regarded than the remonstrances of her greatest warrior and statesman.

---

[1] Annual Register, 1839, p. 545.

[2] Dodson's Admiralty Reports, p. 239.

In order that the provisions of the Act of 1839, which refer to the general statutes as to the slave-trade, should be understood, it may be proper to notice, that, by the Act of 5 Geo. 4, c. 113 (24th of June, 1824),[1] "to amend and consolidate the laws relating to the abolition of the slave-trade," the persons appointed to protect the condemned slaves were authorized to enlist them in the land or naval service, or to bind them out as apprentices for seven years; and, by a subsequent section, orders were to be made when their apprenticeship expired, *so that they might not become chargeable to any colony or parish.* Bounties were given, varying under circumstances, from £20 to £7 10*s.*, for each captured slave, but which were afterwards reduced to £5. By an Act of 1 and 2 Victoria, c. 47,[2] a bounty on the tonnage, of £1 10*s.* per ton, was granted, and £4 additional when there were no slaves; and the Queen's moiety of captures made under treaties was to be paid to the captors.

That the whole British scheme may be considered as to its practical effects on the slave-trade, and that the motives which it holds forth for infringing on maritime rights, in the name of humanity, may be duly appreciated, it is necessary to refer to the arrangements for mixed tribunals under the treaties with Portugal, Spain, the Netherlands, Sweden, and Brazils, and which were afterwards extended to other countries. Each of the two contracting powers was to appoint a commissary judge, and a commissioner of arbitration, and in case the two judges should not agree they were to draw lots for one of the commissioners, who was to decide

---

[1] British Statutes at Large, Vol. LXIV. p. 626.

[2] Ibid. Vol. LXXVIII. p. 224.

conjointly with the judges. And it would seem, that, in the absence of the judge and commissioner of one of the powers, the judge and commissioner of the other were competent to form a court and condemn a vessel whose country was unrepresented. Such was the case as regards The Donna Barbara, which, on other grounds, became a subject of investigation in the Court of Admiralty, without any allusion being made to the composition of the mixed tribunal by which she was condemned.[1]

The slaves were to be delivered over to the government of the country within whose jurisdiction the commission sat, they were to be employed as free laborers, and to receive certificates of emancipation, each government guaranteeing the liberty of the individuals consigned to it. The practical results of this arrangement in Cuba, while there were any cases to be adjudicated, as well as of the use made by the English of the liberated slaves taken by them, either under their general law or the Act of 1839, which has virtually superseded the mixed tribunals, may hereafter be alluded to.

We are now approaching the time when it was to become evident that the policy of the Act of 1839 was intended to embrace all nations, that did not voluntarily submit their vessels to British maritime *surveillance;* and that it may be seen that the Duke of Wellington was not mistaken as to the intended general operation of that act, it may be here stated that it is still in force, though it was, in reference to the negotiation of the Treaty of 10th of July, 1842, with Portugal, specially

[1] Haggard's Admiralty Reports, Vol. II. p. 336; Ibid. Vol. III. App. C, p. 446.

repealed with regard to that country by the Act of 5 and 6 Victoria, c. 114.[1] Indeed in the debate on the original law, it was admitted that American vessels had already in several instances been seized by British cruisers; but it was contended, by the Earl of Minto (the first Lord of the Admiralty), that no exception had been taken by our government or people to the enforcement by them of our own laws against the slave-trade. And on an important occasion in 1843, Lord Aberdeen stated in the House of Lords, that it was only in February, 1841, that Lord Palmerston gave instructions "to abstain from *capturing* American vessels, not *visiting* or *searching* merely, but *capturing*, American vessels suspected to be slavers."[2]

In answer to reclamations, made by the American minister in London for the seizure and detention of vessels belonging to citizens of the United States, Lord Palmerston, under date of August 27, 1841, explicitly claimed a right, and which he avowed the intention of his government to continue to exercise, for British cruisers to examine our vessels, with a view to ascertain by an inspection of papers their nationality, and that they meant that the United States flag should only exempt a vessel from search, when that vessel is provided with the papers entitling her to wear that flag, and proving her to be United States property, and *navigated according to law.*

On Mr. Stevenson's showing that the new pretensions of England, founded on the necessity and expediency of the power, as a means to carry out treaties entered into

---

[1] British Statutes at Large, Vol. LXXXII. p. 980.

[2] Hansard's Parl. Debates, N. S. Vol. LXVIII. p. 659.

with other States, were incompatible with the law of nations as expounded in her own courts, Lord Aberdeen replied, October 13, 1841, intimating that Lord Stowell's decisions were no longer authority, but that the change of circumstances, by the happy concurrence of the States of Christendom, in a great object, "not merely justifies, but renders indispensable, the right now claimed and exercised by the British government." It is, however, due to this nobleman, whose courteous intercourse, during exciting discussions many years ago respecting our north-eastern boundary, is remembered with pleasure, to state, that the tone and manner of this communication differed widely from his predecessor's.

In his note Lord Aberdeen admits that so much respect and honor are due to the American flag, that no vessel bearing it ought to be visited by a British cruiser, except under the most grave circumstances, and well-founded doubts of the genuineness of its character. And he further says: "It is obvious, therefore, that the utmost caution is necessary in the exercise of the right claimed by Great Britain. While we have recourse to the necessary, and indeed the only, means for detecting imposture, the *practice* will be carefully guarded, and limited to cases of strong suspicion. The undersigned begs to assure Mr. Stevenson that the most precise and positive instructions have been issued to her Majesty's officers on this subject."

Mr. Stevenson remarks, in his answer of October 21, 1841, that the claim asserted by Lord Palmerston made the commander of every British cruiser the exclusive judge, whether American vessels were "properly provided with papers entitling them to the protection of the flag they wear and proving them to be United

States property, and navigating the ocean according to law." He alludes to the fact, that, while England claims to herself the dominion of the sea, she was rebuking Hayti for attempting to enforce the principles of her laws and treaties against those States that were not parties to them. He asks: "Why might not the right of search for seamen and deserters, and that of impressment, be defended upon the principles of the present claim? Let it be supposed, for the purpose of illustration, that Great Britain entered into treaties with other nations, by which the right of search for seamen or deserters was given to the vessels of each other, and that some of the contracting States, in order to evade their engagements, should resort to the fraudulent use of the flags of other nations. And suppose also, that, with the view of enforcing those treaties, it should be deemed expedient to assert a right of boarding and examining, upon the high seas, the vessels of nations who had not surrendered the right, and were not parties to the treaties. Does Lord Aberdeen or her Majesty's government believe that such a power would be tolerated by any independent nation upon the face of the earth?"[1] In Lord Aberdeen's answer, which was addressed to Mr. Everett under the date of December 20, 1841, he attempted to make the distinction between *visit* and *search*. "The right of search," he said, "is not confined to the verification of the nationality of the vessel, but also extends to the object of the voyage, and the nature of the cargo. The sole purpose of the British cruisers is to ascertain whether the vessels they meet with are really American." As, however, it was

---

[1] Cong. Globe, Vol. XI. part 2, p. 5–11.

not proposed to abandon the claim to detain our vessels, in order that British cruisers might satisfy themselves, by the "inspection of their papers or other proofs," of the genuineness of their character, the distinction was without any practical difference.

Nor is it to be forgotten, that, if the proposition of the British government was tenable, we were in a much worse position than if we had actually conceded the right of search. In the treaties which England made with the several European powers, there is a limit as to the time when, and the place where, the visitation for the examination of papers may be made; and the right of detention is confined to certain cruisers specially authorized. In our case, if admitted at all, it would be equally competent for any ship of war (and if English ships have the right, all others possess it) to visit and detain any merchantman at any time and in any part of the ocean.

The transfer of the negotiation to Washington prevented any answer from Mr. Everett; but the attempt to bind us by the acts of other States had already been met by President Tyler, who, in his annual message of December 7, 1841, declared that the "United States cannot consent to interpolations into the maritime code at the mere will and pleasure of other governments," and that "when we are given to understand, as in this instance, by a foreign government, that its treaties with other nations cannot be executed without the establishment and enforcement of new principles of maritime police, to be employed without our consent, we must employ language neither of equivocal import nor susceptible of misconstruction. Whether this government should now enter into treaties containing mutual stipulations upon this subject (the slave-trade), is a question for its mature deliberation. Certain it is, that, if the right to detain American ships on the high seas can be justified on the plea of a necessity for such detention, arising out of the existence of treaties between other nations, the same plea may be extended and enlarged by the new stipulations of new treaties, to which the United States may not be a party."

Circumstances, at this time, seemed particularly to favor the British attempt to render her navy as efficient for maritime supremacy in peace as in war. Austria, Russia, Prussia, all of which, as well as France (already bound by the treaties of 1831 and 1833), had so strenuously opposed at Vienna and the subsequent congresses, any general crusade against the slave-trade, now yielded to the diplomacy of England. On 20th of December, 1841, notwithstanding the irritation growing out of the Syrian and Egyptian question, and the isolation in which France was placed by the convention of 15th July, 1840, for regulating the affairs of the East, without her participation, a treaty was signed between them all and Great Britain, "whereby," says the Annual Register, "the former powers agreed to adopt the English laws relating to the slave-trade." The traffic was declared piracy, and the five powers mutually conceded to each other the right of search, in the case of all vessels bearing their respective flags.[1]

In a matter in which the powers other than France had no navigation or commerce to be affected, as the Mediterranean was excluded from the operation of the treaty, it is not so remarkable that they should have

[1] Annual Register, 1841, p. 254.

ultimately yielded to the persistent importunities of England, as that they should have so long resisted her. What, indeed, shows the purely formal character of this convention (and the same remark is applicable to many other slave-trade treaties made by England), is, that the employment of cruisers was in nowise compulsory; and it is not understood that any ship belonging to Austria, Prussia, or Russia was ever empowered to search British or other vessels under the treaty, or that any captures have been made by England of slavers belonging to those countries.

But the convention was not without effect in strengthening the British pretensions. Fortunately, however, for our country, she was then represented in Paris by a minister whose social position, acknowledged intelligence, and political antecedents not only gave him free access to the official organ of the government, but to the King himself, and to those whose opinions exercised a controlling influence over the public sentiment of the nation.

General Cass deemed the occasion to be one which made it his duty to adopt such a course as might tend to arrest a proceeding disastrous alike, as he regarded it, to France and to his own country, united by "a community of interest in the liberty of the seas," "a community of opinion respecting the principles which guard it," and "a community in danger, should it ever be menaced by the ambition of any maritime power." He interposed to prevent the ratification of the Quintuple Treaty by France, by addressing an official note to the Minister of Foreign Affairs, under date of February 13, 1842, having already published, in January, in English and French, a concise examination of the question in discussion between the American and British governments concerning the "right of search."

We learn from his official despatches, that his letter was laid before the King and council, that he had full conversations on the subject, not only with Mr. Guizot but with Mr. Thiers, by the latter of whom he was assured, so early as the 22d of February, that it was "impossible the ministry should ratify the treaty," and that if they did, "they would lose their places." On the 24th of that month, the ratifications of the four other powers were exchanged, in London, without that of France. And in Mr. Guizot's reply to General Cass, May 26th, he entirely repudiates, whatever may be the fate of the treaty or the views entertained by the cabinet of London, any construction which should extend its operations beyond the parties to it.[1]

General Cass was also encouraged in his course by Mr. Dupin, the first lawyer of France, as well as one of her ablest statesmen, who said to him, speaking of the claim of "visit," "Persist in your opposition to that unjust and arrogant pretension. All France is with you."[2]

In the Chamber of Deputies, the amendment of Mr. Jacques Lefebvre to the answer to the King's speech, and which directly referred to the maintenance of the independence of the flag, was carried without a dissenting vote, except from the ministers. And such was the success that attended General Cass's labors, that, when the Chambers adjourned, on the 4th of June, the treaty was virtually dead.

Nor was the defeat of the Quintuple Treaty the only

---

[1] Wheaton's Elements, Lawrence's Introduction, p. cxxi.

[2] Congressional Globe, Vol. XV. p. 627, 628.

result of the discussions of the subject, to which General Cass's efforts had contributed. The debates of the ensuing year (1843) compelled the ministry to take measures for annulling the treaties, by which France was already bound to England, and the application of which, she herself had, by treaties with them, extended to other countries. "The most vehement advocates of freedom," says the Annual Register, "seemed disposed to allow the slave-trade to be carried on with impunity, rather than subject the French flag to an imaginary degradation by conceding the right of search; and, in truth, the very idea that such a right as that contended for by Great Britain could be derogatory to any nation was never entertained in France until the question had been raised by America, which was no party to the treaties of 1831 and 1833, nor to the proposed treaty of 1841, which France, although she at first assented to it, subsequently refused to ratify." The Marquis de Turgot contended for the revocation of the Treaties of 1831 and 1833. Mr. Dupin denounced them as based on English ambition, and having for their object to increase the maritime interests of Great Britain, and to protect and extend her empire over the sea. They were also condemned by the Duke de Noailles and the Prince of Moskowa, and even Guizot admitted that there had been abuses, while he referred to the complications growing out of the treaties with other powers, and to the impossibility of obtaining the consent of England to any modification.[1]

We have been more minute in noticing the Quintuple Treaty than we might otherwise have deemed necessary, in consequence of an impression which has

---

[1] Annual Register, 1843, p. 287].

prevailed that the failure of France to ratify it was owing to the conclusion of the Ashburton Treaty. It is due to history that it should be understood, that the former was effectually defeated before the commencement of negotiations for the latter; though its adoption may not have been without influence in inducing the substitution of the Treaty of 1845 for those of 1831 and 1833 between France and England, and which, though not as objectionable as the ones which it superseded, was itself not wholly free from abnormal exceptions. In fact, the convention of 1845, which, as well as those that preceded it, had been concluded by the Duke de Broglie, was a temporary expedient that France resorted to, in order to extricate herself from obligations which the discussion of the right of search had rendered extremely unpopular. The negotiation of it was distinctly put on that ground, both in the British House of Commons and the French Chambers. Sir Robert Peel said: "Public opinion had been raised in France against the right of search. Hour after hour we receive messages from the French government, and we reply, 'We retain our opinion as to the obligation that is upon us to put down this traffic. We cannot depart from the measures already taken, unless we satisfy ourselves that the French government will adopt some other measure as efficacious in its provisions.'" And Mr. Guizot declared, "He had represented to the British ministry the necessity of devising some other means of attaining the common end—the suppression of the slave-trade—than the right of visitation, which was likely to compromise the friendly relations between the two countries."[1]

---

[1] Annual Register, 1845, pp. 15], 217].

It may not be uninteresting to notice the part taken by Lord Palmerston, then as now out of office, when this subject was under discussion in the House of Commons. He objected to the appointment of a joint English and French commission to consider a substitute for search, declaring that "it is a perfectly self-evident proposition, — no one can doubt it, — that, unless *you have a maritime police*, it is impossible, absolutely and physically impossible, to put down the slave-trade." He treats with no great respect the proposition to have a foreign naval officer to cruise in British vessels, and a British officer on board every French cruiser, saying: "If it is to be done for one power, it must be done for another; so that there would be perfect little Noah's arks sailing about,—naval officers by pairs in these slave-trade cruisers. The idea is perfectly absurd; and any man who intends seriously to propose such a measure as that, means nothing less than to get rid of the treaty altogether, and to render it perfectly inefficient." He did not attach any importance to its unpopularity in France, "as the value of the treaty did not depend on the alacrity, zeal, and ability of French officers, but of our own, nothing effectual having been done towards the suppression of the trade by the naval force of any country except that of Great Britain." To show the tenacity with which he adhered to the right of search, we may quote what he said that the government ought to have declared to France: "We will enter into no negotiation with you upon the subject, unless we contemplate the substitution of some measure for the right of search; we contemplate no such substitution; and we should only mislead you if we held a sham negotiation with you to enable the minister of the day to answer an opposition speech."[1]

In the discussions in the Chamber of Deputies in the session of 1846, the compromise treaty was far from meeting universal satisfaction. Mr. Billault said: "He could not admit that the convention of May 29, 1845, had replaced the commerce of France under the national flag. He must maintain that the faculty to verify the nationality of vessels was an innovation on the maritime rights of France, it was contrary to their fundamental principles; France had never recognized it, and the English had never admitted it either." The Duke de Broglie had said in 1822, that "nations had undoubtedly a right to effect the verification in question in time of war, but in time of peace the right ceased to exist." Benjamin Constant held the same opinion, and in 1829, Laval Montmorency and Polignac protested, in two despatches to the English government, against all attempts to verify the nationality of vessels sailing under French colors. In the negotiations preceding the treaty of 1831, De Broglie and Sebastiani wrote to Lord Palmerston, declaring that "vessels sailing under the French flag could not be regularly seized and proceeded against unless by French cruisers." The acquiescence of Mr. Dupin would seem to have been obtained only because "he supposed that it had the meaning which the American government had attached to the Ashburton Treaty."[2]

It was after the unanimous action of the Chambers, and when it was known that the Quintuple Treaty, so far

---

[1] Annual Register, 1845, p. 19].

[2] Annual Register, 1846, p. 240].

as regards France, had no longer any vitality, that Lord Ashburton was deputed as a special minister to the United States; but though the "right of search" had been put directly in issue in the correspondence of the preceding year, it was not, much to the regret of those who believed that to allow such a pretension to remain unrebuked, after what had already occurred, could not but permanently prejudice our cause, discussed during the negotiation which resulted in the treaty of August, 1842. The attempt to waive it was made by the eighth articles tipulating for the maintenance, by each party for five years, of a separate squadron on the coast of Africa; and by a subsequent article (the ninth) the parties were to unite in remonstrances with other powers, in order that all markets should be shut against the purchase of African negroes.

The eighth article would seem to have been deduced from a system that had been initiated as early as 1840, under an agreement between the American and British commanding officers on the coast of Africa. The correspondence between Mr. Webster and Commanders Bell and Paine were, indeed, the only communications submitted to the Senate in connection with this branch of the treaty. By that arrangement the cruisers of the respective nations were to detain all vessels under American colors, equipped for and engaged in the slave-trade; that, if proved to be American property, they should be delivered to an American cruiser, and if proved to be Spanish, Portuguese, Brazilian, or English property, to an English cruiser. This compact, which not only conceded the English pretensions to the fullest extent, but might well have brought us into collision with other powers, was of course promptly repudiated by President

Van Buren's administration as being not only unauthorized by instructions, but contrary to the established and well-known principles and policy of the government.[1] It was, however, adduced by Lord Palmerston, as a justification for British interference in the case of the American vessels whose detention had been the subject of complaint;[2] and he gave it in the House of Commons, as an apology for those orders to capture our ships which Lord Aberdeen had brought to the notice of parliament.[3]

It would seem from the declaration of Lord Ashburton in the House of Lords on his return from America, that Mr. Webster's silence on the subject had led to an extraordinary delusion, on his part, as to the importance attached to their maritime rights by the government and people of the United States. This was the more extraordinary, considering the part that he himself had taken in the House of Commons as Alexander Baring, in reference to the Orders in Council, prior to the war of 1812. In the discussion on the Queen's speech (February, 1843), Lord Ashburton is reported to have said: "Undoubtedly I went for the purpose of meeting this question, amongst others, which were the subject of complaint. If there was nothing done on the subject from the time I arrived till the time I left, it was because I heard nothing but satisfaction expressed at the last communication of Lord Aberdeen. I left the country with the entire conviction that the ground

---

[1] Secretary Paulding to Lieutenant Paine, June 4, 1840.

[2] Lord Palmerston to Mr. Stevenson, August 5, 1841; Same to Same, same date; Same to Same, August 27, 1841. Cong. Globe, Vol. XI. pp. 2, 5, 7.

[3] Hansard's Parl. Deb. N. S. Vol. LXVIII. p. 1231.

taken by my noble friend was entirely satisfactory."[1] It is not easy to reconcile this declaration with what occurred between Lord Ashburton and Mr. King, as stated, in his place, by that senator.

The injunction of secresy having been removed from their proceedings, we learn not only that the action of the Senate on the treaty was not unanimous, but the reasons of the minority are given in their published speeches.

President Tyler, in his message, August 11, 1842, sustained the provision for the African squadron, on the ground that it was a substitute for visitation and search. "The examination or visitation," said he, "of the merchant vessels of one nation, by the cruisers of another, for any purpose except those known and acknowledged by the law of nations, under whatever restraints or regulations it may take place, *may lead to dangerous results. It is far better by other means to supersede any supposed necessity or any motive for such examination or visit.* . . . . It has been thought, therefore, expedient, not only in accordance with the stipulations of the Treaty of Ghent, but at the same time, as removing all pretext on the part of others, for violating the immunities of the American flag upon the seas, as they exist and are defined by the law of nations, to enter into the articles now submitted to the Senate."

Mr. Benton not only opposed the treaty on the general consideration arising from objections to all entangling alliances, especially to one which might admit the interposition of a foreign power in the execution of our own laws, but on account of the reason assigned by the

---

[1] Hansard's Parl. Deb. N. S. Vol. LXVIII. p. 314.

President for its adoption. "It stands confessed, that our naval and diplomatic alliance with Great Britain is the price which we pay for five years' exemption from search, and for the favor of not being made a party to the quintuple alliance. The alliance with Great Britain is a substitute for these penalties; and a more ignominious purchase of exemption from outrage never disgraced the annals of an independent nation." [1]

To the same effect Mr. Buchanan said: "These articles, then, were entered into for the purpose of removing all pretexts, on the part of the British government, for examining and searching our vessels on the coast of Africa. These articles are the price which we have agreed to pay for the privilege of not being searched by British cruisers."

He further objected: "The treaty itself provides that the two governments shall 'give such orders to the officers commanding their respective forces as shall enable them most effectually to act in concert and coöperation.' The British squadron on the coast of Africa will necessarily be larger than the American; and it will be commanded by an admiral or other officer of high rank. Although no direct orders may be issued from the British commander to an American officer, yet when the two squadrons are bound to coöperate with each other, influence will probably be substituted for command. The American squadron will, in effect, become a mere subsidiary force to that of England. Upon a review of all the considerations involved in this subject, I feel deeply solicitous that the pending motion should prevail, to strike this eighth article from the treaty. The

---

[1] Congressional Globe, Vol. XII. Appendix, p. 12.

honor of the nation requires that we should make the amendment. After all that has passed, we should stand upon the sacred principle of the law of nations, that the American flag, waving at the masthead of an American vessel, shall protect her from visitation and search by British cruisers." [1]

In a memorandum apparently furnished by him, it is stated: "In voting upon the separate articles of the treaty, Mr. Woodbury voted against those in respect to the engagements to furnish a force of eighty guns towards suppressing the slave-trade. This arose not from an unwillingness to do every thing proper for abolishing that trade with alacrity and efficiency, but from an aversion to enter into an entangling alliance with any nation for any object, and from a reluctance to seem compelled by England, or bound to her, to do as to other countries what she had a right to demand or enforce. The attitude appeared, on our part, one of inferiority and submission, or of subjection. A sovereign nation ought to do what is just and honorable as to the world at large, or as to the general interests of humanity, without the intervention or guardianship of any other nation." [2]

It is proper to notice in this connection, that, while Mr. Calhoun would have preferred an informal arrangement for mutual coöperation, he denied that the one entered into was an acknowledgment of the right of search. He considered it, under the circumstances, a surrender of that claim on the part of Great Britain. "It is," he said, "carefully worded, to make it mutual,

---

[1] Congressional Globe, Vol. XII. Appendix, p. 104.

[2] Ib. p. 28.

but at the same time separate and independent; each looking to the execution of its own laws and obligations, and carefully excluding the supervision of either over the other, and thereby directly rebutting the object of search or visitation." [1]

Mr. Rives, chairman of the Committee on Foreign Relations, contended, that the "vital question of the independence of the flag having been disposed of in the unequivocal denial of the right of search, in the President's message, communicating the correspondence between Mr. Stevenson and Lord Palmerston and the Earl of Aberdeen, while rejecting the plans proposed by other governments for this object, we should come forward with one of our own, which should bring the most efficient means to the general extirpation of this odious traffic, without intrenching on the liberty of the seas and the established principles of maritime law." "In virtue of the arrangement each power will separately and independently exercise the necessary supervision and police over all vessels sailing under its own flag, *neither being permitted to visit or search the vessels of the other;* but the presence of the two squadrons, always on the alert and acting in friendly concert, will afford, by their vigilant oversight, complete security against the use of the flag of either power to cover the prohibited traffic, and will, at the same time, give protection to the merchant vessels of each, when necessary, from all unlawful interruption or molestation." [2]

The inference, from an examination of the debate of the Senate, is, that, while a difference of opinion existed

---

[1] Congressional Globe, Vol. XII. Appendix, p. 52.

[2] Ibid. p. 63.

as to the expediency and propriety of purchasing an exemption from its exercise, all united in considering the pretension, on the part of Great Britain, to a right of search, as utterly untenable, and also in the belief that the treaty would, at least during its continuance, prevent the assertion of such a claim.

Among those who voted to erase the eighth article, which motion was lost by a vote of thirty-seven to twelve, were Messrs. Benton, Buchanan, Woodbury, and Silas Wright.[1] The treaty finally passed by a vote of thirty-nine to nine,[2] including in the minority Messrs. Benton and Buchanan, and also Mr. Conrad of Louisiana, who was subsequently a member of Mr. Fillmore's cabinet.

As the next annual message of the President (December, 1842) contained a renewed disclaimer of the pretensions of England, and stated that "the ground assumed in the former message had been maintained, and all pretence removed from interference with our commerce, for any purpose whatever, by any foreign government," Sir Robert Peel, then Prime Minister, on occasion of the opening of parliament, declared: "I am ready, whenever it is necessary, to prove that the doctrine of the right of visitation laid down in the despatch of 1841 has been strictly carried out. With respect to the treaty lately signed between this country and the United States, I say that in acting upon that treaty we have not abandoned our claim to the right of visitation, *nor did we understand that in signing that treaty the United States could suppose* that the claim was abandoned. On the

---

[1] Cong. Globe, Vol. XII. p. 1.

[2] Ibid. p. 2.

contrary, we thought that a step in advance of our object had been taken, when the United States consented to send a naval force for the suppression of the traffic in slaves, though we by no means considered or accepted of that proceeding as an equivalent for any right which we claimed with respect to visitation." In the same speech, he had previously alluded to what he considered "the President's misapprehension that Lord Aberdeen had insisted, in 1841, on the right of *search*, which extends to the cargo and destination of a vessel, instead of the right of *visit* merely to ascertain its nationality."[1]

In the discussions to which Sir Robert Peel's speech gave rise in the Senate (February 23), Mr. Benton thus referred to the discrepancy in their statements: "The evil of this *visitation* is, then, according to the President, now terminated. According to Sir Robert Peel, it is not terminated. And here is the difference, — and a serious one." "What then? Shall our government go on blindfold with the treaty until the case occurs, until an American vessel is searched by a British cruiser, and then negotiate or fight? Shall the government do this, — and it is the fate of weakness to wait for events, instead of guiding them, — or shall it stop and clear up the difference at once?" He was in favor of stopping all action under the clause of the treaty until the two governments agreed as to its meaning. General Jackson, he remarked, had in October, 1834, directed Mr. Forsyth to say to Sir Charles Vaughan, on this very point of a convention for the suppression of the slave-trade, that "the government of the United States was

---

[1] Annual Register, 1843, p. 14].

definitively decided not to become a party to any convention on the subject of the slave-trade." "This was the answer of General Jackson," he said. "It is an American answer." Mr. Benton added, that he would not go into the question of the identity between search and visitation. "Stopping a vessel on the high seas, he understood to be firing a-head of her and over her and then through her, if she does not stop. This was a rude process, even if for an innocent purpose; and he was against subjecting American vessels to be so stopped by English cruisers."

Mr. Archer, who had become chairman of the Committee on Foreign Relations, did not contend that the right of visitation had been formally renounced; but only that all occasion for the exercise of that right had been removed.

Mr. Allen asked, If Great Britain did not surrender her right to search our vessels, why did we agree to spend half a million a-year for the purpose of searching our own? According to Sir Robert Peel, visitation was not now confined to the slave-trade, but extended to the whole world of commerce. He considered the course of England a declaration that the treaty was to be utterly disregarded.

Mr. Calhoun said that it was impossible for any man to read the treaty and say that the right of visitation was not superseded by its provisions, — certainly the right of visitation on the coast of Africa.

Mr. King said that it was proposed by the government to adopt a course which would supersede the necessity of British visitation to ships bearing our flag on the African coast, — to execute the right of search ourselves in relation to vessels hoisting our flag. The eighth article of the treaty proves that the arrangement was thus accepted by Lord Ashburton, as superseding the necessity for the British right of visitation; for it points out the very mode in which vessels shall be visited. He had seen the version of Sir Robert Peel's speech in the London Times. It bore the impression that he maintained not only the British right of visitation in the general sense, but in a sense which would extend to the coast of Africa. If such was his meaning, it was a palpable violation of the treaty. We had agreed to do what, as an independent nation, we were bound to do,—to carry into effect our own laws, and therefore there no longer remained a pretence for England to persevere in her claim of a right of visitation. Had he not considered this point clearly settled, he never could have voted against striking out that article in the treaty. He firmly relied on its being a suspension of the British claim, and that it was so stipulated by Lord Ashburton, who had himself told him that that was the case.

Mr. Benton said the treaty had been ratified upon the President's view of it; and if there was an attempt to reconcile the message to Sir Robert Peel's speech, it would be a fraud on the senators who voted for it.[1]

The British government, lest any inference should arise that their late plenipotentiary had disavowed the right of search, directed their minister, Mr. Fox, to read to the Secretary of State a despatch from Lord Aberdeen, in which it is stated, that, "from the principles which she had constantly asserted, and which are re-

---

[1] Congressional Globe, Vol. XII. p. 330.

corded in the correspondencé between the ministers of the United States in England and herself in 1841, England had not receded, and would not recede."

The purport of Lord Aberdeen's despatch was communicated to the House of Representatives, in a report of the Secretary of State to the President, of 27th of February, 1843. The President, in his message, says: "I regarded the eighth article as removing all possible pretext on the ground of mere necessity, to visit and detain our ships upon the African coast because of any alleged abuse, by stipulating to furnish an armed force, regarded by both the high contracting parties as sufficient to accomplish that object. Denying, as we did and do, all color of right to exercise any such general police over the flags of independent nations, we did not demand of Great Britain any formal renunciation of her pretension; still less had we the idea of yielding any thing ourselves in that respect. We chose to make a practical settlement of the question." The Secretary says "that the right of search never formed the subject of discussion during the late negotiation, and that no concession was required by the United States, nor made by Great Britain."

In the debate on the ensuing day (February 28), for carrying the treaty into effect, Mr. McKeon objected to it as not settling all questions, especially the claim of the right of visitation set up by Great Britain, and which had always been opposed by the United States. Since the last war the British government had been assiduously endeavoring to extend their naval power, and to acquire the right to superintend the police of the seas.

Mr. Cushing sustained the construction of the treaty,

as given by the President in opposition to that of the English Prime Minister. On the despatches of Lord Aberdeen and the speech of Sir Robert Peel, he assumed that all pretext for any right of search was taken away, except what was conceded by that treaty. The negotiations and legislation of England, with regard to the right of search, went hand in hand. The act of parliament in 1839, giving to British cruisers unlimited authority to detain and search vessels suspected in any manner of being engaged in the slave-trade, and the Quintuple Treaty, contained the same provisions *totidem verbis.* Sir Robert Peel conceded all that was asked in regard to the belligerent right, and also as regards the conventional or reciprocal right of search; but said that there was a right to *visit,* distinct from the right of search, which he declared would be assumed and exercised. In all books of international law the right was termed "*droit de visite.*" If the boarding officer might go behind the flag, why not also behind the papers to the ship's crew and cargo? Either the assumed right of visitation was a nullity, or it was the right of search under another name. Mr. Cushing therefore denied the construction of Sir Robert Peel, and affirmed that of the President. He added: "He was of opinion that we had cause to regret that we had entered into any sentimental legislation. The only delicate point in this matter was a question in the law of nations, which might arise upon the piracy act of Congress. It was a false step, he considered, on our part, to enact the piracy law with regard to the slave-trade."[1]

Mr. Webster's instructions to Mr. Everett of March

[1] Cong. Globe, Vol. XII. p. 368.

28, 1843, examined the whole question with an ability and an extent of research that increase our regret, that, from any circumstance, our country should not have had the benefit of the argument at the opportune period.

The eighth and ninth articles, Mr. Webster considered a mutual stipulation for concerted efforts to abolish the slave-trade, but that "this stipulation has no other effect on the pretensions of either party than this: Great Britain had claimed as a *right* that which this government could not admit to be a *right*, and in the exercise of a just and proper spirit of amity, a mode was resorted to which might render unnecessary both the assertion and the denial of such claim."

As Lord Aberdeen had, in his despatch to Mr. Fox, stated, "that, if in the exercise of this right (of visit), either from involuntary error or in spite of every precaution, loss or injury should be sustained, a prompt reparation would be afforded," Mr. Webster shows the inconsistency of this suggestion with the claim as made by England. "The general rule of law," he says, "certainly is, that, in the proper and prudent exercise of his own right, no one is answerable for undesigned injuries. It may be said that the right is a qualified right; that it is a right to do certain acts of force at the risk of turning out to be wrongdoers, and of being made answerable for all damages. But such an argument would prove every trespass to be matter of right, subject only to just responsibility. If force were allowed to such reasoning in other cases, it would follow that an individual's right in his own property was hardly more than a well-founded claim for compensation, if he should be deprived of it. But compensation is that which is rendered for injury, and is not commutation, a forced equivalent, for acknowledged rights. It implies, at least in its general interpretation, the commission of some wrongful act."

And again: "Any detention of an American vessel by a British cruiser is a wrong, a trespass; although it may be done under the belief that she was a British vessel, or that she belonged to a nation which had conceded the right of such detention to the British cruisers, and the trespass therefore an involuntary trespass. If a ship of war, in thick weather, or in the darkness of the night, fire upon and sink a neutral vessel, under the belief that she is an enemy's vessel, this is a trespass, a mere wrong; and cannot be said to be done under any right, accompanied by responsibility for damages. So if a civil officer on land have process against one individual, and through mistake arrest another, this arrest is wholly tortious; no one would think of saying that it was done under any lawful exercise of authority, subject only to responsibility, or that it was any thing but a mere trespass, though an unintentional trespass. The municipal law does not undertake to lay down beforehand any rule for the government of such cases; and as little, in the opinion of the government of the United States, does the public law of the world lay down beforehand any rule for the government of cases of involuntary trespasses, detentions, and injuries at sea; except that in both classes of cases law and reason make a distinction between injuries committed through mistake and injuries committed by design; the former being entitled to a fair and just compensation, the latter demanding exemplary damages, and sometimes personal punishment."

As a conclusion from the preceding statement, Mr.

Everett is instructed that the government of the United States does not admit, that, by the law and practice of nations, there is any such thing as a right of visit, distinguished by well-known rules and definitions, from a right of search." [1]

The question of visitation was, after the receipt of this despatch in England, a copy of which was given to Lord Aberdeen, several times alluded to in parliament. Lord John Russell having, on one occasion, remarked that the President had said that the meaning of the whole article was a total abandonment of the right of visit, Sir Robert Peel replied: "From the despatch of December 20, 1841, government would never depart; that despatch stated in the most conclusive manner their views, and it was Lord Ashburton's instructions; — that despatch was unanswered. Lord Ashburton had no authority to concede more." [2]

Lord Stanley (now Earl of Derby), the then Minister for the Colonies, on the 2d of May, speaking on a vote of thanks to Lord Ashburton, moved by Mr. Hume, said: "The continued excitement on the question of the slave-trade had been owing to the insulting terms in which Lord Palmerston had insisted on rights which, in no degree, had been abandoned by Lord Ashburton. Lord Aberdeen did not think it necessary to tell the American government in a public despatch, 'that the English government was not bound to take notice of every bit of bunting sewed up into the form of an American flag.' Lord Aberdeen put forth 'visit' as a right which should be exercised at the peril of the

---

[1] Webster's Works, Vol. VI. p. 340.

[2] Hansard's Parl. Deb. N. S. Vol. LXVIII. p. 324.

party exercising it. If by a detention without a reasonable ground of suspicion, a British vessel stopped an American vessel, even proceeding upon an illegal commerce, which they had no right to stop, the American government could claim and the British government would make compensation, not for the exercise, but for the abuse, of the right. The United States did not recognize the right, but agreed that 'visit' might be exercised, subject to certain conditions."

Sir Robert Peel said the difference between the present and former government is, "If we visit American vessels, we do it on our responsibility and are liable to make compensation, if we make a mistake. Lord Palmerston captured American vessels, knowing them to be *bonâ fide* American."[1]

In the House of Lords, thanks to Lord Ashburton were moved, April 3, by Lord Brougham, who by the virulence of the invective with which he assailed him manifested the extent of General Cass's services in defeating the Quintuple Treaty. The Marquis of Lansdowne opposed the motion, because after the President's message he could not think the question of search put on satisfactory ground. He trusted that the government would persevere in claiming the right to visit *all* vessels, for the purpose of seeing whether the flag they bear is genuine or not. If instructions to that effect are given, it will bring the matter to an issue. "I think that it should be known in America as it is here, that our cruisers, when they meet an American flag, have the power, when they see just cause of suspicion, to stop the vessel for the purpose of searching it. Till

---

[1] Hansard's Parl. Deb. N. S. Vol. LXVIII. p. 1190.

I see the President admitting that he considers such suspicion a sufficient justification for the right of search, I cannot see that the disposition of men to peace and good-will will be promoted by this negotiation. Nothing is so likely to disturb it as a confused understanding of this important right in America."

Lord Brougham. "The President admits the right."

Lord Lansdowne. "He does, but not the exercise of it."

The Earl of Aberdeen. "I confess, though I always thought it the greatest object of this country to obtain a mutual right of search, on that point this treaty is a very considerable advance towards the abolition of the traffic. The plan was proposed by the last government, through Mr. Fox, in 1839. When we visited an American vessel, it was because we thought it belonged to a State that had given us permission by treaty. Without such treaty we have no right to visit any vessel. The President argues that we do not claim it as a perfect right. It is not such a right as all nations have in apprehending pirates, but it is a right, the exercise of which is accorded by treaty. And it is because we have reason to believe that a vessel belongs to a country with which we have a treaty that we have any ground for visiting her, with a view of ascertaining her nationality. Now, such being the nature of our pretensions, we shall adhere to them in spite of all opposition. I must say that I think the United States had cause to complain of the pretensions put forth at no distant period, and enforced. Before exercising the right, there must be ground for suspecting that the vessel is engaged in the slave-trade, and belongs to a state with which we have a treaty of search. If an American is visited, reparation must be made. The American squadron will have no right to visit any but American vessels."

Lord Campbell contended that the right of visit was a perfect right, and that it existed by the law of nations. He said that Lord Stowell had reference to the right of search, and not the right of visit. He regarded the eighth article as a retrogression, and that it effected nothing.

Lord Denman would not enter into the distinction between *search* and *visit*, but he stood up for the right of prevention.[1]

The instructions issued by the British government were dated 12th of December, 1843, and were consequently drawn in accordance with Lord Aberdeen's exposition of the right of visit, and though, when cruising in coöperation with the United States squadron, the commanders are told that they "will do right" to leave to the American commander to take the first step to visit a vessel having the colors of his country, and ascertain her right to wear that flag; yet they are to make the search themselves if they suppose the delay of our officers will enable her to escape unvisited. The British officers are authorized to "require the suspected vessel to be brought to, in order that the nationality may be ascertained," and they are instructed that they "will be justified in enforcing" the order by coercive measures, if necessary; and as they are impliedly directed to proceed to the most minute searches, if not satisfied by the "vessel's papers or other proof of her nationality," it is obvious that it has, at all times, depended on the greater or less stringency with which

[1] Hansard's Parl. Deb. Vol. LXVIII. p. 604.

the orders (complicated as they are with the instructions relating to vessels of countries with which England has treaties according search) are carried out, whether collisions took place or not.[1]

In the message of December, 1844, President Tyler refers to the cases of seizures and detentions of American ships on the coast of Africa, "upon the mistaken supposition, indulged in at the time the wrong was committed, of their being engaged in the slave-trade," and for which England had admitted her obligation to make compensation. Several reclamations also grew out of the West India emancipation, and the attempt to apply to vessels of the United States, having slaves on board, involuntarily entering the ports of the British islands, through stress of weather, mutiny, or otherwise, the new municipal code, and thus to establish a police over vessels passing from one American port to another.

This matter had been ably discussed in the Senate of the United States by Mr. Calhoun in March, 1842, and the resolutions proposed by him, declaring the seizure of slaves under those circumstances a violation of the law of nations, were unanimously passed. The British government granted compensation in the cases where the slaves were liberated before the passing of the act abolishing slavery, but refused it for those that arose subsequently. No provision was made for the latter cases by the Treaty of 1842, though Mr. Webster addressed Lord Ashburton a note on the subject, under date of August 1, 1842. They were, however, with those arising from seizures on the coast of Africa, compensated for, under the convention of 1853 between the United States and

---

[1] Cong. Doc. 28th Cong. 2d Sess. H. R., No. 150, p. 116.

Great Britain, for the settlement of outstanding claims of the citizens of either country against the other, that had arisen since the Treaty of Ghent. And thus the principle was established by an international tribunal, binding at least as between England and the United States, that, as vessels of a country, when on the ocean and beyond the territorial limits of any other nation, are subject to its exclusive jurisdiction, so they only pass under the jurisdiction of a foreign state, when they *voluntarily* enter its ports. It was distinctly decided in the case of the "Creole," which, as being connected both with murder and mutiny, had attracted particular attention, that, as she was on a voyage sanctioned and protected by the laws of the United States, and by the law of nations, her right to navigate the ocean could not be questioned, nor, as growing out of that right, the right to seek shelter or enter the ports of a friendly power, in case of distress or any unavoidable necessity. A vessel navigating the ocean carries with her the laws of her own country, so far as relates to the persons and property on board, and, to a certain extent, retains those rights even in the ports of the foreign nations she may visit.[1]

At different periods, going back as far as 1823, our flag had been subjected to annoyances, in reference to the fisheries on the eastern coast of America, secured to us by the convention of 1818, which was a compromise

---

[1] Report of Commission of Claims, p. 244. Of the $329,734 awarded to American claimants, $301,848 were for cases referred to in the text. See also, on this subject, Calhoun's Resolutions and Speeches, Congressional Globe, Vol. VIII. Appendix, 266; Wheaton's Elements of International Law, Lawrence's Introduction, p. cxxix.; Webster's Works, Vol. VI. p. 303; Benton's Thirty Years, Vol. II. p. 282.

of our claim under the Treaty of 1783. There had been repeated diplomatic discussions on the subject, and Mr. Forsyth, in instructing Mr. Stevenson, February 20, 1841, stated as the point of difference, that the provincial authorities assume a right to exclude American vessels from all their bays, including the Bays of Fundy and Chaleurs, and to prohibit their approach within three miles of a line drawn from headland to headland, while the American fishermen believe that they have a right to take fish anywhere within three miles of land. Certain relaxations in the pretensions of England, were, in 1845, announced by Lord Aberdeen to Mr. Everett; but the whole subject obtained renewed importance in 1852, on account of a British force being ordered to that coast to protect the claims of the colonists, and a correspondence involving the original merits of the controversy was carried on at London and Washington, without result.[1] The Treaty of June, 1854, has settled the rights of the respective parties on a new basis, but as regards previous reclamations, as in the case of the vessels driven into West India ports, the decision of the commission, under the convention of 1853, was favorable to the United States. The arbiter, in awarding compensation for a vessel employed in fishing in the Bay of Fundy, that had been captured, in 1843, and condemned in a British Vice-Admiralty Court, decided "that the Bay of Fundy is not a British bay, nor a bay within the meaning of the words, as used in the Treaties of 1783 and 1818."[2]

The course adopted in 1845, and pertinaciously ad-

---

[1] Wheaton's Elements, Lawrence's Ed. p. 238, note.

[2] Report of Commission of Claims, p. 186.

hered to, with regard to Brazil, presents one of the strongest cases that can well be imagined, of an attempt to control, by municipal legislation, matters exclusively belonging to a foreign and independent sovereignty. This case was even more flagrant than that of Portugal in 1839. The Treaty of 1817 with Portugal, by which Brazil had bound herself in 1826, had expired by the operation of its own provisions, in March, 1845, and that fact, including the termination of the mixed commissions, as the Emperor announced to the legislative chambers, had been fully notified to the British government. In August of that year an act of parliament, 8 & 9 Vict. c. 122, was passed, by which jurisdiction was given to the British courts of admiralty to take cognizance of any vessel carrying on the African slave-trade in contravention of the Treaty of 1826, and the same provisions were applied to Brazilian vessels as to British-owned. The pretence for this usurpation is stated, in the statute, to be derived from the provision of the convention, that, at the expiration of three years from its ratification, "it should not be lawful for the subjects of the Emperor of Brazil to be concerned in carrying on the slave-trade under any pretext whatever, and that the carrying on of such trade after that period by any subject of his Imperial Majesty should be deemed and treated as piracy."[1] Under this act English cruisers have been authorized to enter the creeks and harbors of Brazil, cut out any vessel that they might deem a slaver, and subject her to be tried, not even by a mixed tribunal, but by one exclusively English. And yet, though the slave-trade with Brazil has confessedly ceased, Lord

[1] British Statutes at Large, Vol. VIII. p. 1059.

Palmerston last year objected to the repeal of this statute.[1]

Nor is it an unimportant matter to notice the claim, put forth in this connection, on behalf of England, that Brazil, having once agreed with her by treaty that the slave-trade should be deemed and treated as piracy, she had a right, after the expiration of the treaty, to punish as pirates by the common law of nations, all Brazilians who might be engaged in the traffic. Indeed, one of her commentators on public law contends that England dealt very leniently with Brazil, in only capturing and condemning her ships and cargoes, instead of trying her subjects in her courts and hanging them for piracy by virtue of an act of parliament.[2]

The right to arrest pirates can have no connection with the present inquiry. Cases of that nature, not growing out of the statutory enactments against the slave-trade, do not often occur, and when they do, it does not appear that the guilty parties have obtained any impunity from the principles adopted by the United States in reference to the flag. No one would allege that any suspicion of ordinary piracy gave rise to the

---

[1] Hansard's Parl. Deb. Vol. CXLV. p. 309. This disregard of the sovereignty of an independent State has not remained a dead letter on the statute-book. Among other cases of the unwarrantable exercise of British power, in January, 1850, the Cormoran, an English frigate, took in sight of land and burned, without any process of law, with its cargo and papers, after having landed the crew, the Brazilian ship Santa Cruz, which had left St. Sebastien on the 2d of the month, bound to Rio de Janeiro. To a complaint of the Brazilian minister of foreign affairs, the British chargé d'affaires replied, that the Santa Cruz had been taken for being engaged in the illicit traffic of slaves, and had been destroyed, because she was found incapable of keeping the sea till she could be brought to the next vice-admiralty court. — De Cussy, Droit Maritime, tom. 2, p. 270.

[2] Wildman's International Law, Vol. II. p. 152.

detentions and seizures which led to the discussions of 1841, nor has it been supposed that the collisions in the Gulf of Mexico, which have been the subject of recent discussion, arose from any apprehension of a return of the aggressions on the commerce of the world, effectually suppressed thirty years ago by the American navy, though not without a technical violation of the territorial sovereignty of Spain, rendered necessary by her unpardonable neglect to maintain the police of her own coasts. But the right to detain a vessel on suspicion of piracy, even with the peril of being deemed a trespasser in case the suspicion proves groundless, is confined to those charged with that offence, as known to the law of nations, — to those who are universally regarded as *hostes humani generis*. Pirates are the enemies of every country and at all times, and as with them there is no state of peace, they are always subject to the extreme rights of war, among which is that of visitation and search.

No justification, on the plea of searching for pirates, can, however, be offered for detaining an American vessel, on suspicion of her belonging to a country, which had granted to England a reciprocal right of search, and of her being engaged in the slave-trade, to which, by a legislative perversion of language, the term piracy is applied. This is a proposition which it is important not to overlook. The principle that no two or more nations can, by an agreement between themselves, impose disabilities on another nation, not a party to the compact, or create new rights in their own favor, was sufficiently elucidated, when a contrary doctrine was assumed by Lord Aberdeen. It need scarcely be affirmed, that nothing that would not have justified or palliated the detention of a vessel before the anti-slavery treaties were concluded, and when the slave-trade was held a legitimate commerce by all the world, can now authorize the stopping of a foreign merchantman. Hautefeuille alludes to it as a proof of the little practical difficulty likely to arise from seizures based, *bonâ fide*, on the suspicion of piracy, that no treaty refers to the subject.[1]

Nor can the claim of visitation on the high seas be sustained by the practice which has prevailed of exercising an inquiry for fiscal or defensive purposes, in the neighborhood of the coast and beyond the prescribed jurisdictional limits of a nation, such as the hovering laws both of the United States and England authorize.[2] "This," says Lord Stowell, "has nothing in common with a right of visitation and search upon the unappropriated parts of the ocean." And he adds, "a recent Swedish claim of examination on the high seas, though confined to foreign ships bound to Swedish ports, and accompanied in a manner not very consistent or intelligible with a disclaimer of all right of visitation, was resisted by (the British) government as unlawful, and was finally withdrawn." [3]

That no apprehended inconvenience, on account of the revenue or even public safety, can, in time of peace, give a *right* of visitation on the high seas, although near the coasts of a country, if beyond the ordinary maritime jurisdiction, but that such power can only be exercised by the positive or tacit permission of the State to whose subjects the merchantman belongs, is well

[1] Hautefeuille — Droits des Nations Neutres, tom. 3, p. 489.

[2] See United States Statutes at Large, Vol. I. p. 700.

[3] The Louis, Dodson's Admr. Reports, Vol. II. p. 246.

shown by an eminent civilian of Doctors' Commons, in an opinion which he has recently furnished for the guidance of a foreign government.

Having alluded to the American case of the Marianna Flora, as establishing the principle that the State which authorizes, by her municipal laws, her cruisers to effect such seizures, incurs a responsibility towards foreign powers in executing such laws, and that if any other State should remonstrate, and resist their application, she must withdraw her claim to enforce them, Doctor Twiss adds: "In ordinary cases, indeed, where a merchant ship has been seized on the high seas, the sovereign whose flag has been violated waives his privilege, considering the offending ship to have acted with *mala fides* towards the other State with which he is in amity, and to have consequently forfeited any just claim to his protection." As, however, in the case before him, Sardinia did not assent, but claimed a restitution of the vessel taken under her mercantile flag, the King of Naples cannot, he asserts, set up the provisions of his own laws as an answer to a claim made under the law of nations. Lest it might be supposed, that, in this view of the law, a State would be helpless to check or punish outrages on its coasts which do not amount to piracy committed by vessels under the mercantile flag of another State, if such vessels can only escape in time on the high seas, before the cruisers of that State fall in with them; the remedy for such an anomaly, which, he says, is in practice more ideal than real, is found in the *comity of nations*. The privilege of the flag is the privilege of the State; and when there is *mala fides* in the wrongdoers, the State through courtesy waives its privilege, and either permits the State which has been injured to avenge the breach of its laws, through its own tribunals, or will assist it to obtain redress against the wrongdoers before the courts of their own country, if they have in any way made themselves amenable to punishment for a breach of their own laws.[1]

That the right of visitation and search, as it was asserted by Lord Palmerston and Lord Aberdeen, cannot exist, in time of peace, independent of treaty, is established as well by institutional writers as by the practice of nations. It would, of course, be in vain to seek for authorities at the time that England herself was looking to conventional concessions as the sole means for its exercise, and instructing her cruisers, that, being a belligerent right, it had ceased with the war.

The American publicist Wheaton (who is himself the author of a standard work on the "Right of Search," and whose "Elements of International Law" is now received as the text-book in the great law schools of England), writing, as minister at Berlin, to the Secretary of State, July 6, 1843, says: "The right claimed (by the English) comes to this,—a right to seize and send in for adjudication, before the court of the captor's country, subject to the payment of costs and damages, in case of seizure without reasonable cause. I do not know what Lord Aberdeen and Sir Robert Peel's admiralty lawyers may have told them; but I defy them to show a single passage of any institutional writer on public law, or the judgment of any court, by which that law is administered, either in Europe or America, which will justify the exercise of such a right on the high seas in time of peace."[2]

---

[1] Opinion of Dr. Travers Twist, London Times, April 1, 1858.

[2] Wheaton's Elements, Lawrence's Introduction, p. cxxiv.

Among the French writers of established reputation who have alluded to the British pretensions are Hautefeuille, Ortolan, and Massé. The liberal views of the first-named commentator as to the immunity of merchant vessels, even as against belligerents, have been already noticed. His distinction between "visitation and search" (*la visite et la recherche*), it will be remembered, is for the benefit, and not for the detriment, of the neutral.

Hautefeuille says that the right of visit (even restricted as it is by him, in war) cannot exist in peace, being a power conceded to the belligerents for the exercise of belligerent rights. The special treaties which grant the reciprocal right in time of peace, go beyond what he deems even the belligerent claim, and accord a right of *search.* He considers the treaty with France, of 1845, an illustration of the right of *visit,* as he defines it, while those of 1831 and 1833 were instances of the right of *search.* It can hardly be necessary to mention, that all conventions of this character are earnestly opposed by him as containing (even that of 1845) flagrant violations of the principles of international law. "In time of peace," he says, "the flag of a ship is the sign of its nationality, not merely *primâ facie,* but absolutely, for all foreign ships. The cruisers of the nation to whom the flag belongs have exclusive jurisdiction over it, including the power of verification and inquiry (*enquête*). The only exception is in case of piracy. As to the words, 'the slave-trade and other unlawful commerce,' of which the treaty of 1845 speaks, they are without meaning. The slave-trade is not an unlawful commerce on the part of a Frenchman, except so far as French laws make it unlawful. It is only so with respect to France.

What I say as to the slave-trade I say of all other kinds of commerce, without exception. In time of peace there is not any unlawful commerce as regards foreign States, unless the individual or the vessel that is carrying on the trade is within the custom-house limits, upon the territory and under the jurisdiction of the foreign State. This principle is absolute, and admits of no exception." *Visit*, in time of peace, has only been invented, he remarks, by England, since 1815, to injure the navigation of other countries, and is an outrage on the national dignity and independence.[1]

Massé, cited by Hautefeuille, says, that, "whatever may be the object of *visit*, in time of peace, it is always an act of police, which cannot be exercised by one nation towards another, because it implies, on the part of the visitor, a sovereignty, incompatible with the reciprocal independence of nations. Furthermore, two nations cannot advantageously grant one another, by special conventions, the reciprocal right of visit in peace. The appreciation of the utility of conventions of this nature is undoubtedly a political question. But it is certain, that, as such conventions imply an abandonment of the sovereignty, which is, in its very essence, inalienable, and incapable of being parted with, the two nations which have mutually given up their rights can only have made a temporary abandonment of them, which no lapse of time can render definitive."[2]

Ortolan says that he agrees with all the authors on international law, and especially with the American publicist, Wheaton, that "the right of visitation and

---

[1] Hautefeuille — Droits des Nations Neutres, tom. 3, p. 471–487.

[2] Massé — Droit Commercial, liv. 2, tit. 1, c. 2, § 2.

search cannot exist in peace, except by special treaty." He likewise says that it is an international usage very often practised, for ships that meet at sea to hoist their flag to show their nationality, and to interchange salutations. Speaking of this usage, he had said, in his first edition, "that there existed in favor of ships of war, in reference to merchantmen, a right of inquiry as to the flag (*droit d' enquête du pavillon*). By this expression, which is probably new, the word right (*droit*) should not be taken in its most extended sense. But when this right is exercised by a ship of war in reference to a foreign merchantman, it does not precisely mean a right of compulsion, and the correspondent obligation is only a moral obligation." [1]

De Cussy also says, "The right of visit, as recognized and tolerated by the usage of nations, does not exist in time of peace. *Le droit de visite* is exclusively a belligerent right." "The extension of the exercise of the right of visitation and search, in time of peace, if the great maritime States (acting under the influence of a sentiment of humanity and equity which does honor to the sovereigns who signed the treaties concluded with a view to the abolition and extinction of the slave-trade) continue to show themselves too easy in the adoption of the measures considered the most efficacious by England; the extension, we say, of the right of visitation and search, in time of peace, will be the commencement of a system for the dominion of the seas, by means of the abuses to which visitation and search would give rise, by confounding, intentionally, all the distinctions of times and circumstances, of peace and war, and all

---

[1] Ortolan—Diplomatie de la Mer, 2eme ed. tom. 1, p. 258, 262.

the rights applicable to the two different situations, the one regular, the other forced and temporary." [1]

Elsewhere he remarks, speaking of the resistance to the right of search: "The United States manifested under these circumstances, in the highest degree, the sentiment of respect, which every nation ought to feel for the independence of its flag, and for its own dignity as a sovereign state. The other powers, carried away by the philanthropic sentiment which induced them to sign the treaty of 1841, seem to have forgotten that they were favoring the strongest passion of England, her dominion of the sea. Was it not to go in advance of all her hopes to accord to her numerous ships of war a right of visitation and search, in time of peace, in exchange for the same right received by the very inconsiderable military marines of Russia, Austria, and Prussia, and of the other maritime States which acceded to the treaty of 1841?" [2]

Phillimore, the most eminent among the recent English commentators, is evidently embarrassed by an effort to reconcile the new doctrine, which he gives, in the words of Lord Aberdeen, with the principles of international law, or with the opinions of previous publicists. In this he is aided, as will hereafter appear, by a note unfortunately inserted in the later editions of Chancellor Kent's commentaries. He does not, however, distinguish, by any definition susceptible of application, between *visit* and *search*, but he says that "it is quite true that the right of visit and search is a strictly belligerent right. But the right of visit, in

---

[1] DeCussy — Droit Maritime, tom. 2, p. 385.
[2] Ibid. p. 364.

time of peace, for the *purpose of ascertaining the nationality of a vessel*, is a part indeed, but a very small part, of the belligerent right of visit and search." Again, he says: "This right of mitigated visit, in time of peace, is sometimes delicately described as the *right of approach*. It is called by the French *droit d'enquête du pavillon*, as distinguished from the *droit de visite ou de recherche*; and it is said that this *nationality of the flag* may be ascertained by signals and hailing, and that, even when there is a suspicion of piracy, all proceedings beyond the exchange of hailing and signals, must be taken at the risk of the man-of-war who visits. Whether these limitations be just or not, it is unquestionable that the *visit* for the purpose of ascertaining the nationality of the vessel must be exercised without the right of *search*, which is exclusively incident to a belligerent."[1]

It may also be noted, that Dr. Phillimore being likewise called on, on behalf of the Sardinian government, for his opinion, as a jurist, in the case of the Cagliari, in which Dr. Twiss was consulted, cites, as an authority for denying the right of a Sicilian frigate to seize a *bonâ fide* Sardinian vessel on the high sea, Wheaton's "Right of Search." He alludes, at the same time, to the question, as to the right of visitation as distinguished from search, which he says had been formerly much discussed between Great Britain and the United States, but which did not necessarily arise in that case. He not only contends, that, if any offence against the Neapolitan government had been committed by the Cagliari, redress should have been sought by an application to Sardinia,

---

[1] Phillimore's Commentaries upon International Law, Vol. III. p. 418, 420.

but he also denies the right of seizing on the high seas and treating a foreign vessel as a pirate, because, though her nationality is otherwise established, she may not have on board all the papers required by the internal legislation of her own country.[1]

It is believed that sufficient has been stated to show, before the recent occurrences in the Gulf of Mexico, which have attracted anew the attention of Europe and America to this most interesting question of international law, a systematic effort, on the part of Great Britain, to establish a police of the ocean, which might eventuate in her being recognized as the exclusive maritime power of the world. In this object she had been efficiently aided by the zeal which philanthropists of all countries have, during the last half century, manifested for the suppression of the African slave-trade; while the only barrier to her complete success has been the United States, who have not only themselves maintained the freedom of the seas, but, by their interposition with France, prevented the propositions of England from being adopted as the common law of Europe. The submission of America was alone wanting, and to effect that, as the Duke of Wellington intimated, the legislation of 1839 was directed. And when it is remembered, that, according to Lord Palmerston, it is in the competency of the boarding officer to determine whether any vessel that he *visits* is *navigated according to law* (a matter implying a knowledge of our navigation laws), it is evident that the examination which the British govern-

[1] Documenti diplomatici communicati al Parlamento nazionale dal presidente del Consiglio dei ministri relativi alla vertenza col governo di Napoli per la cattura del Cagliari.

ment proposed to enforce, placed our whole mercantile marine under the supervision of her navy. Not to have required, in 1842, as preliminary to all other negotiations, a renunciation of the pretension, was, we have ever conceived, a most unfortunate mistake; and the article of the convention providing for a separate squadron by each nation on the coast of Africa, aggravated, instead of diminishing, the evils of the omission.

According to Phillimore, there were in 1849, twenty-four treaties in force for the suppression of the slave-trade between Great Britain and other civilized powers, including those with the United States and France, ten of which established mixed courts, and the others (with the exception of the two conventions specially mentioned) likewise accorded a mutual right of search, though they required the captured vessel to be handed over to the tribunals of the country under whose flag she had been taken.[1] The States stipulating for mixed commissions were the Netherlands, Sweden, Brazil (whose treaty had expired, as she contended), Spain, Portugal, the Argentine Confederation, and the republics of Uruguay, of Bolivia, of Chili, and of Ecuador. These courts would seem for some years to have ceased exercising practically any jurisdiction. In fact, by excusing one power after another from the obligation to maintain cruisers, which were in some cases dispensed with in the original treaties, England had obtained almost exclusively the police of the African seas. It is more advantageous to the British officers to make captures under the statutes of 1839 and 1845, — those statutes by which the general *surveillance* of the ocean

---

[1] Phillimore on International Law, Vol. I. p. 253.

was assumed, — than under the treaties; and as the condemnation then takes place in the Vice Admiralty courts, without exposing the slave-dealer to personal penalties, the subjects of other countries, whether of those that have treaties with England or not, are not unwilling, when complete success fails them, that the felony should be commuted by a trial in the British court, where loss of property is the worst evil that can await them.

The commissary judge at Sierra Leone writes to Lord Palmerston, under date of December 31, 1848: —

"Owing to the operation of the Acts of 2 and 3 Victoria, c. 73 (1839), and 8 and 9 Victoria, c. 122 (1845), no vessel has been brought into the mixed courts during 1848, but a very large number have been adjudicated in the Vice Admiralty Court of this colony. That some of the vessels were really Spanish property (though under the Brazilian flag), I cannot doubt; but the now general system of destroying ships' papers, &c., previous to capture, effectually conceals their nationality. This is doubtless caused by the penal law promulgated at Madrid on 2d of March, 1845, which law seems to have struck the slave-traders with terror, for during the two years only one vessel, under the Spanish flag, has been adjudicated in the mixed courts of Sierra Leone.

"During the past year no case was brought before the British and Spanish, British and Netherlands, British and Chilian, British and Bolivian, British and Argentine, British and Uruguay, mixed courts of justice.

"During the year there were condemned in the Vice Admiralty Court under 5 Geo. IV. c. 113, 2 and 3 Victoria, c. 73, and 8 and 9 Victoria, c. 122, thirty-one vessels, fourteen of which were captured under the Brazilian flag, and fifteen were without ship's papers or colors, one under the British, and one under the flag of the United States."[1]

There was the same absence of business in the mixed courts in 1855,[2] the cases being all carried to the Vice Admiralty Court, where a larger amount of prize money is obtained by the captors. Thus, by means of parliamentary enactments, have British tribunals acquired jurisdiction over vessels of all nations. Nor has there been any exception as regards the United States, the operation of whose penal laws has been defeated by the intervention of British naval officers and British courts; while the very impunity which England accords, through the interference of her cruisers, to the individuals engaged in the slave-trade, is the foundation for the constant crimination of the United States for a supposed connivance at the traffic.

Commander Powell complained, in April, 1850, to Captain Hastings of the British navy, of the seizure of vessels of the United States by the authority of the latter. The American note is given as furnishing a practical illustration of the construction put by their officers on the English instructions, a copy of which was inclosed in Captain Hastings's reply. Commander Powell says: "The vessel is American in model, an American claims to be her master, as also her mate and crew in part are American, the papers are exhibited, the log-book opened, all under her proper flag, but the foreign boarding officer is not yet satisfied as to her

---

[1] Parliamentary Papers, 1849.

[2] Parliamentary Papers, 1856, Vol. LXVIII.

nationality. There are suspicious Brazilians about the deck, and he demands a further scrutiny and finds the vessel prepared to receive, or actually full of slaves. In the mean time, the master is alarmed, hauls down the American flag, destroys his papers, declares he is not the captain, calls out a Brazilian, who invests himself with office as the captain. All this, in some cases, in the presence of the British officer, who seizes the vessel as Brazilian, and discharges the delinquents. He *adjudicates* the case, as far as the American parties are concerned, and perhaps wrongfully — certainly, so far as the suppression of the slave-trade is concerned; and this is the only object for which our government expends the treasure and sacrifices the lives of our people on the coast so freely — wrongfully, for the probabilities are that the destroyed papers are genuine documents, which, produced in evidence against the parties before the United States tribunals, would subject them to the heavy penalties of the laws prohibiting the slave-trade — wrongfully, for the parties, be they who they may, are not held to answer for their crimes."[1]

In October, 1857, the American brigantine Bremen was boarded by Commodore Wise, of the British government steamer Vesuvius, who informed her commander that it was his intention to take the vessel, that he did not wish to see her papers, at the same time giving him his choice to be taken under the American flag or otherwise. The colors were hauled down, the papers thrown overboard, the vessel seized as a prize "without colors or papers." That this was a systematic procedure is apparent from the answer of the Brit-

[1] 31 Cong. 1 Sess. Senate, Ex. Doc. No. 66, p. 9.

ish commodore to a lieutenant of the United States ship Dale, then cruising in the neighborhood. He did not deny, that, in the event of his meeting with an American slaver under American colors and having genuine papers, he would use means to induce the captain to throw the papers overboard. This assumption by the British cruisers of the appropriate functions of the American squadron was very recently the ground of a formal remonstrance by Commodore Conover to the British Admiral, "as being an interference with the rights of Americans to take and bring to punishment those who, while they wear the flag of the United States, offend against their laws, as being in violation of the express stipulations of the two governments to enforce their laws for the suppression of the trade separately and respectively, and of the often expressed declarations of the American government, that the American flag shall protect American property from all intrusion of foreign cruisers."[1]

The same course has, however, been continued to the latest period, as may be inferred even from the notes of the present British minister at Washington to the Secretary of State.[2]

The convention of 1845 between England and France is no longer operative. It contained a provision, that if, at the end of the tenth year, the preceding conventions, of 1831 and 1833, were not reëstablished, they should be considered as abolished. Some time before its expiration, the stipulated number of cruisers, which had been twenty-six, was reduced to twelve. The actual

---

[1] 35 Cong. 1 Sess. Senate, Ex. Doc. No. 49, p. 35, 39.

[2] Ibid. p. 10.

obligations of France, as regards the right of search and her legislation respecting the slave-trade, are thus stated, in the *Revue des deux mondes* for the 1st of January: —

"It is not generally known, that the treaties respecting the right of visitation and search (*droit de visite*) have ceased to exist. The famous conventions which excited such clamorous divisions in the political world have expired unnoticed. Those of the 30th of November, 1831, and of the 22d of March, 1833, contained no clause limiting their duration; but that of 29th of May, 1845, which was signed after warm parliamentary discussions, and which impliedly abrogated the preceding ones, was only to remain in force ten years. By the terms of the tenth article, which fixes this limit, the negotiations for its extension were to be resumed in the course of the fifth year, that is to say, in 1850. We cannot say whether negotiations took place at the appointed time; but we are certain, that the present government has purposely allowed the period of expiration, of 29th May, 1855, to arrive, without desiring that the question should be again taken up. Now, then, all this exceptional system is at an end, and there is no other international law on this subject except that which results from the great political Treaties of 1814 and 1815, which proclaim, in general terms, the abolition of the trade, but leave every people fully at liberty to employ whatever means they think proper to accomplish it. The legislation which has been with us the consequences of these diplomatic acts is to be found entire in the *ordonnance* of January 8, 1817, and in the laws of April 15, 1818, April 25, 1825, and March 4, 1831. It is useless to say that nothing in this legislation authorizes the interference of a foreign power in our proceedings."[1]

But though the eighth article of our convention of 1842, might, by the terms of the treaty, have been made to cease at any time after 22d August, 1847, which was five years from its ratification, it still continues in force; and its execution, on our part, despite all that has been done by British cruisers to render useless our African squadron, was, so late as December 24, 1857, made the subject of an official note from Lord Napier to General Cass. That communication is referred to in this connection on account of the issue, which it seems purposely to have raised, by the renewed assertion of the right of search, or visit. Averring that many vessels engaged in the slave-trade had hoisted American colors, Lord Napier says, "this precaution does not protect the slaver from *visit*, but it exonerates him from *search*."

General Cass, concentrated in his reply of April 10, 1858, the arguments which had been so effective in France, sixteen years before, with the results of experience and recent investigation. He declares that "the distinction taken between the right of visitation and the right of search, between an entry for the purpose of examining into the national character of a vessel and an entry for the purpose of examining into the objects of her voyage, cannot be justly maintained upon any recognized principle of the law of nations." "The United States deny," he repeats, "the right of cruisers of any power whatever to enter their vessels by force in time

---

[1] Revue des deux mondes, Janvier 1er, 1858, p. 96.

of peace, much less can they permit foreign officers to examine their papers and adjudicate upon their nationality and whether they are navigated according to law. No change of name can change the illegal character of the assumption. Search or visit, it is equally an assault upon the independence of nations." These positions were, in addressing a British minister, most aptly sustained by a reference to the statesmanlike speeches of the Duke of Wellington and the unanswerable reasoning of Lord Stowell.

General Cass answers the argument deduced from involuntary mistakes, by distinguishing between an accidental or unintentional trespass, and the doing of an act under claim of right, so frequently confounded in the British documents. He well meets, as he did in his letter to Mr. Guizot, the suggestion that certain antislavery treaties could not be carried out, or, as Lord Aberdeen added, English laws enforced against English subjects, without boarding American vessels.[1] And on this point, we may again turn to the judgment in The Louis: "It is no objection to say that the British may by disguise elude the obligations of British law. The answer of the foreigner is ready, that you have no right to provide against that inconvenience by imposing a burden upon his navigation. If even the question were reduced to this, that either all British ships might fraudulently escape, or all foreign ships be injuriously harassed, Great Britain could not claim the option to embrace the latter branch of the alternative. When you complain that the regulation cannot be enforced without the exercise of such a right, the answer again is,

[1] 35 Cong. 1 Sess. Senate, Ex. Doc. No. 49, p. 49.

that you ought not to make regulations which you cannot enforce without trespassing on the rights of others." [1]

The reply of General Cass very opportunely anticipated a revival of the system of boarding and searching our vessels, which this time was the more offensive in consequence of its being practised on one of our great commercial highways. General Cass's first note on this new subject of complaint was written on the fourth of May. The British minister answered it on the sixteenth; but he did not seem to have had any special information respecting the operations, though it has since appeared that the transferring of the cruising ground from the coast of Africa to the Gulf of Mexico was the result of a deliberate decision of the British government. Indeed, there is an extraordinary coincidence in the fact, that, both on this occasion and when the difficulties occurred which preceded the Ashburton Treaty, the obnoxious proceedings took place in consequence of the orders of Lord Palmerston, who left it to his successors to allay the excitement which he had caused.

Instructions were sent to Mr. Dallas on the twelfth of May, informing him of an outrage by a British armed vessel, the facts of which he was directed to communicate to Lord Malmesbury, and to express to him the earnest desire of the President that this practice, which seemed to be once more prevalent, of detaining and searching American vessels, should be discontinued; and that the most peremptory orders should be given for that purpose. "Whatever may be the true object," it is

---

[1] Dodson's Admiralty Reports, Vol. II. p. 254.

added, "of the voyage of The Cortes, as she had papers stating her American character, she was subject to neither search nor capture by the British cruiser." [1]

On the eighteenth of May, General Cass again wrote to Mr. Dallas, transmitting to him a list of vessels, which had been forcibly detained and searched in the Gulf of Mexico. He also stated, that "in addition to these aggressions on the high seas, and indefensible acts of violence against several of our merchant vessels, a forcible entry and examination has been committed by a British steamer in the harbor of Sagua la Grande, in the island of Cuba." Proper representations, he is told, will be made as to these cases to the government of Spain, and if protection is not afforded by it from lawless violence to vessels resorting to Spanish ports, it must be found in the power of our country. The President expects that the officers who have been guilty of the outrages shall be held responsible for their conduct, and that just pecuniary compensation will be made to the parties for all injuries. Mr. Dallas is directed to call Lord Malmesbury's particular attention to the occurrence at Sagua la Grande.[2]

---

[1] The Cortes has already been condemned in the Vice Admiralty Court of Jamaica. A letter from Kingston under the date of May 28, announcing that event, and which is published at New York, in the *Courrier des Etats Unis*, says: "This vessel, though evidently built in the United States, could not present regular papers, and was brought in here. She has been decided to be a good prize. What diminishes greatly, even in the opinion of the most violent adversaries of slavery, the honor which the English cruisers seek to acquire by such captures, is, that the commander, other officers, and even the crew, have an exorbitant share from these prizes. Officers are every day seen who in three or four years have enriched themselves by a business which ends in becoming piracy, rather than a philanthropical work."

[2] In time of war, when a ship has been captured in neutral territory, it is only the neutral that can question the validity of the capture. The enemy

On the twenty-eighth of May, the Committee on Foreign Relations of the Senate, through their chairman, Mr. Mason, made a report, which stated that "American vessels, pursuing the paths of lawful commerce on the high seas, or passing near the American coast from one domestic port to another, under the flag of their country, have been pursued, fired into, and compelled to stop, by the public force of a foreign power; questioned as to their destination, their cargo, and the character of their crew; required to submit to an examination of their sea-papers and to a scrutiny into the objects and purposes of their voyage," and that others anchored at the port of Sagua la Grande, in the Island of Cuba, have been subjected to a police inquisition by the same foreign power.

The committee say that the documents accompanying the President's message disclose the fact, that these acts of visitation and examination of American vessels were sought to be justified, under the plea of necessity for the suppression of the slave-trade. They will not go into any inquiry as to such alleged necessity. The assent of the United States, though often invoked, has never been yielded to any such system of police on the seas. There is no right of visitation, far less of search, to be exercised in time of peace by any nation of the ships or vessels of other nations, nor can there be, so long as the laws of the civilized world touching the freedom of the

---

has no rights whatever against a captor, and if the neutral sovereign omits or declines to interpose a claim, the property is condemned *jure belli* to the captor. (The Anna, 3 Wheat. 447.) But the principle of the preceding rule has no application, it is conceived, in peace, and the claim which Spain has on England, and which the United States have on Spain, does not impair our right to demand redress directly from England.

sea are respected by civilized men. Neither is there any distinction to be drawn in the claim of *right* between visitation at sea by the armed vessels of a foreign power, when unattended by examination and search, and when so attended. The offence and violation of public law consist in the *visitation* without regard to its purpose, when claimed as a *right* against the will of the party subjected to it. Were it otherwise, there would follow, of course, the correlative right to arrest and detain the vessel until the visitation is effected.

The committee concluded by reporting the following resolutions, which were, on the 16th of June, unanimously adopted by the Senate.

"*Resolved* (as the judgment of the Senate), That American vessels on the high seas, in time of peace, bearing the American flag, remain under the jurisdiction of the country to which they belong, and therefore any visitation, molestation, or detention of such vessels by force, or by the exhibition of force, on the part of a foreign power, is in derogation of the sovereignty of the United States.

"*Resolved*, That the recent and repeated violations of this immunity, committed by vessels-of-war belonging to the navy of Great Britain in the Gulf of Mexico and the adjacent seas, by firing into, interrupting, and otherwise forcibly detaining them on their voyage, requires, in the judgment of the Senate, such unequivocal and final disposition of the subject, by the governments of Great Britain and the United States, touching the rights involved, as shall satisfy the just demands of this government, and preclude hereafter the occurrence of like aggressions.

"*Resolved*, That the Senate fully approves the action

of the executive in sending a naval force into the infested seas with orders 'to protect all vessels of the United States on the high seas from search or detention by the vessels-of-war of any other nation.' And it is the opinion of the Senate, that, if it become necessary, such additional legislation should be supplied in aid of the executive power as will make such protection effectual."

The Senate, it will be remembered, is associated with the President in the treaty making power, and as two thirds of the members present must concur in any conventional arrangements, their views may always be regarded by foreign governments as conclusive on a question of international polity.

In the discussion of the resolutions there was not a senator who implied that visitation or search in any form was admissible or would be tolerated. On the doctrinal points they all adopted the principles as maintained by the Secretary of State, and in the report of their committee. Nor was there any difference among them arising from sectional or party considerations. Among those most inclined to the strongest measures were senators most opposed to the extension of slavery, and who were never considered as supporters of the administration; while Mr. Hammond of South Carolina and Mr. Crittenden of Kentucky, both representing slave States, were the most moderate in their denunciation of the British aggressions.

Mr. Crittenden said: "I do not want any negotiations with Great Britain about the right of search or visitation. That is a subject which is exhausted; our minds are made up on that question, and we do not wish that the government of England should understand that we consider the question on our part open for any argument.

We have made up our minds on it. We only wish to negotiate with her about these acts. When she refuses to make reparation for them, then we will decide whether they are of consequence or importance enough either to our honor or to our interest to make them cause of war. Great Britain may be perfectly willing to renounce these acts and disavow them; and that is all that we have a right to demand. I should think it unworthy of this government to enter into any negotiation on the subject of visitation or search." [1]

Mr. Seward, of New York, needed no law-books or judicial decisions to instruct his mind in regard to the rights of nations upon the great public highways. A nation was to be governed by similar rules that would be applied to an individual. If, because there are thieves and robbers in society, a private citizen can be stopped and searched in the street by every person who may choose to exercise the right of police, then it is true that one nation has a right to constitute itself a police upon the high seas for the purpose of ascertaining the honesty, integrity, and good conduct of other nations; but there is no such right anywhere. It is a claim founded in force, and not in right. The United States have never recognized this right, and never will; and it has been practically abandoned by Great Britain ever since the close of the last war. The true principle is this: as there may be pirates at sea, as well as culprits on land, any person who may choose to challenge another as being an unjust and dangerous person, may either arrest or detain him, but he does it at his peril. If the person proves to be a culprit, he is abandoned to the hands of

---

[1] Cong. Globe, 1857–8, p. 2530.

justice; but if he turns out to be innocent, then the person arresting him is the aggressor, and is bound to give satisfaction. This principle is applicable to nations as well as individuals; and on this principle we ought to demand satisfaction from the government of Great Britain.

Mr. Hale, of New Hampshire, moved to amend the resolutions, by inserting a clause declaring that these acts are belligerent in their character, and should be resisted at all hazards and by all the power of the country.

Mr. Wilson, of Massachusetts, moved to amend the amendment of Mr. Hale by adding the following:— "And the President is hereby authorized and empowered to employ the naval force of the United States, and send the same to the scene of the recent outrages, with instructions to capture the ships which have committed, or which may commit, these belligerent acts."

Mr. Douglas, of Illinois, stated that he concurred in the general tone of the report, but he would make one reservation. Instead of contenting ourselves with an expression of an opinion that this thing must stop, he believed we should bring forward some practical legislation, and authorize and empower the President to stop it. He could see no use in these Resolves. We resolved upon the subject forty years ago, and we have resolved ever since, when these rights have been violated. England has been informed, as formally and solemnly as it is in the power of one nation to inform another, that this invasion of our rights must cease, and if not, that we shall resist by force. What good has it done? England had violated this right thirty-three times, he believed, within the last four weeks; and now shall we say that if she does it a dozen times more, or thirty-three times more, we shall not like it? He presumed that England knew now that we did not like it. What good will it do now to resolve again that this is a violation of our rights, that it is offensive to us, and we shall not submit to it. He believed that there was a more direct way of getting at it, and that was to clothe the President with power to put an end to this course of proceeding; and then, whenever our rights shall be again violated, let him instantly avenge the wrong on the spot. The better mode would be for one of our ships-of-war to get upon the track of the Styx, or any other British vessel that has been committing these outrages, follow her, capture her, make prisoners of all on board, and bring the vessel into an American port to answer for the offence. If the British government avows that act, it becomes an international question between this country and Great Britain; and if she disavows it, it is for us to say what punishment shall be inflicted upon those lawless persons who are then abandoned by their own government as pirates.

Mr. Mallory, of Florida, moved to amend the resolutions by striking out all after the word "resolved," and inserting a substitute to the effect that the recent proceedings of the British naval officers in the Gulf of Mexico and upon the high seas, in forcibly arresting and examining vessels of the United States, owned and navigated by American citizens, and engaged in lawful trade, are without justification or palliation, and an aggression upon the rights of the American people, which they can never suffer to be infringed; and the President of the United States is authorized to adopt immediate measures to arrest at once the continuance of such outrages.

On another day, he said that he felt satisfied that the instructions under which the searches were made were issued in 1844, and that they have never been modified or extended, but that the British officers, impelled by a desire for prize money, as a matter of course, are executing these orders very zealously, and the great number of instances which have occurred about the same time have directed our attention to them. They have been going on for ten years past, and therefore have not attracted so much notice. Mr. Mallory then read a paper issued from the last administration, but not printed, in reference to the American vessel *El Dorado*, fired into by a Spanish frigate. The orders from the Secretary of the Navy were, that, "if any officer of a ship-of-war be present when an outrage of the character mentioned is perpetrated on a vessel rightfully bearing our flag, he will promptly interpose, and relieve the arrested American ship, prevent the exercise of the assumed right of visitation and search, and repel the interference by force." And, in a communication from the Secretary of State, (Mr. Marcy), it is said that "the conduct of the commander of The Ferrolano in firing into an American vessel and subjecting her to visitation and search had been brought to the notice of the Spanish minister, as an act, which, if done by the order of Spain or sanctioned by her, must be regarded as the assertion of a right to exercise a police over our commerce upon the ocean, which will be resisted at every hazard by the government of the United States." [1]

Mr. Hayne, of South Carolina, thought the resolutions were wise, dignified, manly, and proper. He approved

---

[1] Cong. Globe, 1857–8, p. 3054.

the promptness that characterized the conduct of Oliver Cromwell and Andrew Jackson, and expressed the opinion that our interests and honor would be safe in the hands of our gallant navy.

Mr. Toombs, of Georgia, would vote for a resolution, not only to send our force there to prevent these things in future, but to seize these vessels, with or without the authority of the British government. He believed the military force of the country should be placed at the disposal of the Executive, and that we should either sink these aggressors upon our rights, or seize them and bring them to condign punishment. He would be satisfied with nothing short of that.

Mr. Hammond, of South Carolina, differed in opinion with the senator from Georgia. He thought there was much substance in these resolutions, and if they were earnestly maintained by the Senate and the country, they would accomplish the desired object. It was not a small thing to adopt such resolutions; he thought they would result in war, because he did not believe England would abandon the right of search which she claimed. Still he was not in favor of making a declaration of war by a side blow. If it was the intention of this country to go into a war with England, we ought to make a formal declaration of war. It was a momentous matter to engage in a war with that power, and it should be done with all proper form. He believed we had just and ample cause for war, for we had received a most flagrant insult; but he preferred by passing these resolutions to give England one chance to avert an event, which, whenever it occurs, will change the whole face of human affairs.

Mr. Benjamin, of Louisiana, said, the right of visitation cannot be yielded to any nation, without placing in her hands a dangerous power, and least of all can we yield it to such a nation as Great Britain. It is admitted by all writers on international law to be a belligerent right. He thought that the present was a time for the Executive to assert our rights with an energy, which would be more acceptable to the people of the United States than any amount of that diplomacy under cover of which our rights had hitherto been eluded by England.

Mr. Bayard, of Delaware, pointed out an error, favoring the British pretensions, which did not exist in any of the anterior editions of Chancellor Kent's Commentaries, but which, interpolated as a note to the edition of 1844, has been retained in all those subsequently published.[1]

Chancellor Kent's text, which is unchanged, declares that "it (the right of visitation or search) is founded upon necessity, and is strictly a war right, and does not rightfully exist in time of peace, unless conceded by treaty." At the end of a note to the fifth edition, in 1844, purporting to give a summary of the controversy between the United States and England, it is said: "The intervisitation of ships at sea is a branch of the law of self-defence, and is, in point of fact, practised by the public vessels of all nations, including those of the United States, when the piratical character of a vessel is suspected. The right of visit is conceded for the sole purpose of ascertaining the real national character of the vessel sailing under suspicious circumstances, and is wholly distinct from the right of search. It has been termed by the Supreme Court of the United States, the *right of approach* for that

---

[1] Cong. Globe, 1857–8, p. 3059.

purpose (The Marianna Flora, 11 Wheaton, 1, 43); and it is considered to be well warranted by the principles of public law and the usages of nations."[1]

The Marianna Flora, so far from favoring the inference here assumed, has not only been cited in this essay to show that the right of visitation and search does not belong to the public ships of any country in time of peace, but it was one of the authorities relied on to sustain the immunity of merchantmen, in the opinion furnished by Dr. Twiss to the Sardinian government, in the case of The Cagliari. Nor is the authority of The Marianna Flora the less valuable for our purpose, because the judgment of the court was pronounced by Mr. Justice Story, who, in a case in his own circuit (before the law had been authoritatively settled in the Supreme Court, in The Antelope, in conformity to the opinion of Lord Stowell), had manifested a disposition to recognize the doctrine of the earlier English cases in preference to that of The Louis.[2]

In the editions published since the death of Chancellor Kent, which occurred in 1847, the *Quæstiones Juris Publici* of Bynkershoek are also named as a further authority for this note. The work is thus cited: "Bynk. Q. J., Pub. lib. 1, c. 114, s. p." The reference, though it is repeated in successive editions, is undoubtedly intended for c. 14, as there are but two books in this treatise of Bynkershoek, each of which contains twenty-five chapters. The first book is entitled *De rebus bellicis*, and was translated by Mr. Duponceau as "A Treatise on the Law of War." Chapter fourteen treats "of enemy's

---

[1] Kent's Commentaries, Vol. I. p. 153, note *a*.

[2] Mason's Reports, Vol. II. p. 409. La jeune Eugénie.

goods found on board of neutral ships." Speaking, of course, in reference to belligerent rights, it is said "that it is lawful to detain *a neutral vessel*, in order to ascertain, not by the flag merely, which may be fraudulently assumed, but by the documents themselves which are on board, whether she is really neutral."[1]

It is evident that there is nothing in the above quotation which justifies visitation or search in time of peace; and, to put at rest all reliance on the Dutch publicist as an authority for English pretensions, which were he living he would have resisted, it may be added, that though the second book, entitled *De rebus varii argumenti*, is applicable to a time of peace as well as war, the twenty-first chapter, which is the only one that refers to vessels, treats of the salutes of ships of war at sea. It is, moreover, confined to a discussion of the equality of states, and to the claims, such as that of England to the British seas, interposed by some nations to a sovereignty over parts of the ocean beyond the ordinary conceded jurisdiction.[2]

That we have not dilated unnecessarily on what is merely a verbal inaccuracy in a standard work, all will admit when it is considered that the authority of the Commentaries is not only universally recognized at home, but that the distinguished civilian, whose definition of the British claim of visitation we have given, deems himself justified by the note in question in adducing, as an authority for the application of Bynkershoek's belligerent rule to a time of peace, "no less a jurist than Mr. Chancellor Kent."[3] We cannot afford to have arrayed against us, by an oversight of annotators,

---

[1] Bynkershoek, Duponceau's Trans. p. 110.

[2] Bynk., Q. J. P. Ed. Lugduni, 1751, p. 340.

[3] Phillimore on International Law, Vol. III. p. 419.

in addition to one of the greatest names of our country, that of Bynkershoek. This explanation is also due to Dr. Phillimore. An American writer, in a notice of the pending controversy, referring to the third edition of Kent's Commentaries, and relying on the plain language of the text, ascribes to the learned English commentator an unauthorized reference.[1]

The proceedings in parliament, on the receipt of intelligence from America, disclosed, what had been generally believed here, that the recent aggressions had not been the result of new instructions, but merely of the more stringent application, usual on the arrival of cruisers on a new station, of those which have already been noticed as having been drawn up at the end of the year 1843. Lord Palmerston, whose ministry was not terminated till February of this year, admitted that the orders for transferring the cruisers from the coast of Africa to that of Cuba were given by his administration; and he says that the arrangement was adopted "in deference to the frequently expressed wishes of parliament, and in consequence of the repeated deputations which came to members of the late government urging that course."[2]

Fortunately, the present Premier is one of the very few statesmen of England who have a practical acquaintance with America. Thirty-five years ago, as Mr. Stanley, he made an extensive tour of the United States, and though a very young man, he left a most agreeable impression on those who then directed our public councils. On more than one occasion, he, as

[1] Brief Examination, &c., of the Right of Detention, Visit, and Search, by Richard S. Coxe, LL. D. p. 26.

[2] Debates, June 10, 1856.—London Times.

well as Lord Malmesbury, has shown that he was not ignorant of the important economical considerations which cannot be overlooked, even for the interests of the parties intended to be specially benefited, in the application of any extended scheme of philanthropy. The condition in which forced emancipation had placed the West Indies was moreover the object of a personal investigation by his distinguished son, the present Lord Stanley, now, as Minister of the Colonies, his associate in the administration, and who, in 1850, published an account of the deplorable state in which he found the liberated negroes, as well as the Jamaica planters.[1] The tone of the remarks of the Earl of Derby, incidentally referred to in the debate on the declarations of the congress of Paris, and on the difficulties attempted to be settled by the Ashburton Treaty, sufficiently indicate sentiments towards the United States very different from those ever manifested by Lord Palmerston. And on occasion of the enlistment question and the dismissal of the British minister at Washington, his influence was exerted, in the House of Lords, to prevent any unfavorable consequence from those proceedings, which he, moreover, deemed justifiable on our part, to the friendly relations of the two countries. Though Lords Derby and Malmesbury held respectively the same positions that they now occupy when the tripartite convention was proposed in 1852, the sending of a large force the preceding year to the Gulf of Mexico, under pretence of maintaining a police for the protection of Cuba against unauthorized adventurers, was, like the

[1] For a notice of the Hon. Mr. Stanley's letter to Mr. Gladstone, see Quart. Rev., January, 1851, Art. V.

late movement, the act of their predecessors; while though in the case of the fisheries, which came up under their administration, there was no accordance as to ultimate rights, there was a prompt disclaimer against giving any new practical extension to asserted claims.

Nor was it an unfortunate circumstance as regards our reclamations, that the point of international law involved was not abruptly presented to the notice of the British government. The case arising between Sardinia and Naples, threatening, at least, the peace of the Italian peninsula, and in which England through the illegal imprisonment of two of her subjects was incidentally involved, had recently received the attention of the law-officers of the crown. And though there was not an unanimity of opinion on all points arising from the temporary possession of the vessel by Neapolitan rebels, the attorney-general, basing himself on Lord Stowell's authority, in The Louis, and which was thus prominently brought to view, declared that no suspicion even of past unlawful conduct would justify the seizure, in time of peace, on the high seas, by a public armed ship of one country, of a vessel belonging to another.

The first notice in parliament of the aggressions in the Gulf of Mexico was not calculated to induce the hope, that, however desirous the British government might be to avoid all collisions with ours, there would be a concurrence on a principle of international law, which Mr. Webster and Lord Ashburton did not venture to discuss. When Mr. Fitzgerald (Under Secretary of State for Foreign Affairs) was interrogated in the House of Commons, on the 1st of June, regret for the occurrences was accompanied by the declaration, that "the government had sent out instructions to the British officers engaged in the waters of Cuba to exercise with the greatest caution the powers intrusted to them." And the Washington Union, in commenting on Mr. Fitzgerald's speech, remarked that "this language is somewhat equivocal; if it means any thing, it is a declaration that the government intend to pursue the practice itself, but to impose upon its agents 'the greatest caution' and circumspection in its exercise."[1]

On the 8th of June, the Earl of Clarendon, the late Minister of Foreign Affairs, in inquiring of his successor whether he could impart any information as to the rumors from America, said that he "did not see how, unless some right of search was given, the real nationality of the flag of suspected vessels could be ascertained. Such a right had been admitted by all maritime nations for their common protection, for without it the most atrocious deeds might be perpetrated, and yet remain unpunished. But the possession of such a right was a very different thing from the exercise of it."

The Earl of Malmesbury is reported to have answered: "I entirely agree with what my noble friend has said as to the American flag being constantly prostituted to cover the slave-trade, and other illegal acts, and I think it is highly desirable that some agreement should be made between the two countries by which it may be distinctly understood what proceedings ought to be taken by their officers respectively for effectually discovering the impositions to which I have alluded, and which will not be offensive to honest traders. It is to that point I have directed the attention of the

---

[1] Union, June 20, 1858.

government of the United States, and that no later than in a conversation which I had this morning with the American minister; and I think I may say there has not been any great difference of views between us. After that conversation has been reported to the United States government, after the delivery of the despatch which I have written to Lord Napier, and after the orders that have been sent to our officers in those seas, I hope there will be no repetition of such acts as have been described to us, whether truly or not. In these circumstances, I feel that this country need remain under no apprehension that any thing will occur to break the alliance that so happily exists between the two countries."

The Earl of Hardwicke said, in reference to the naval part of the subject, that the mode of operations for inquiring into the nationality of a vessel had been clearly laid down; and if there had been any excess of those instructions, it was against the direction that no offence was to be given to any nation in conducting the operations in those seas.

In the debates in the Lords on the 17th, and in the House of Commons, of the 18th, of June it appeared that the government, having taken the opinions of the law-officers of the crown, had determined to yield the doctrine of the right of visit, without insisting on the preliminary adoption of any conventional substitute.

Lord Brougham referred anew to the distinction between search and visit. He thought that no man could deny that the right of search was a belligerent right; but, making that admission, he was of opinion that ships of any country, not merely slave-dealers but actual piratical robbers, should not be enabled to carry on their nefarious proceedings with impunity, by hoisting a certain piece of bunting.

The Earl of Malmesbury, in reply, said that he did not demur to the doctrines laid down by the noble and learned lord; but as the noble and learned lord had stated that there was a difference between the right of search and visit, he must say that the United States positively, categorically, and constantly had refused to admit the distinction, and the doctrine laid down by the United States was adopted by other countries.

Not long ago he endeavored to obtain from all civilized countries some agreement, by which British officers might know exactly how far they could go in cases of strong suspicion, and be protected by the agreement. He was anticipated by the French government, which laid down this law, — that, in time of peace, no French ship should be detained or searched or boarded, but that certain forms should be gone through without detaining the vessel, which, to a certain degree, though to a small degree, might enable the nationality of the ship to be ascertained, and her right to the flag she carried. He had no reason to conceal what he had done since recent events. *He had admitted the international law as laid down by the American Minister for Foreign Affairs, though not, of course, without being fortified by the opinions of the law-officers of the crown,* but, having admitted that, he had put it as strongly as possible to the American government, that, when it was once known that the American flag covered the cargo, every pirate and slaver on the face of the sea would carry the American flag, and that, instead of the honor of the country being vindicated, that very fact must bring dishonor on the Amercan nation, if an obstinate adherence to its present declarations were persisted in, and the American flag would be prostituted to the worst purposes. He had urged that it was necessary in these civilized times that there should be, if not a right by international law, some agreement among the maritime States as to how far their officers might go to verify the nationality of vessels and the legality of their flag.

He earnestly hoped, from the language he had used, and from conversations he had had, with the American minister in this country, and also from perusing the able paper drawn up by General Cass on this point, that a change of this kind might be agreed upon with the United States, so that, by instructions given to naval officers, the flag of the country might be verified without the risk of offence. Of course, their lordships would not require him to go more into detail as to the great practical difficulties in the way of the suppression of the slave-trade, but he thought a mistake had been committed in sending our squadron to the Cuban waters, instead of keeping it on the African coast. He was told that at the beginning of the Russian war the slave-trade was very nearly extinguished; but during that war a great portion of the squadron was withdrawn from the coast of Africa, and the slave-trade made great progress.

The Earl of Carlisle knew that even such a purpose as the suppression of the slave-trade must be carried on with some reference to changing circumstances and conditions, and he felt convinced, that, in the interval of its suppression, care should be taken that we did not exceed the limits of our well-defined rights, or encroach on the rights or prerogatives of others.

Lord Wodehouse said he was convinced, that, no matter what instructions were given to our officers, if we undertook, by an armed squadron, to visit and examine the great number of American vessels which passed through these waters, sooner or later serious differences with the United States would occur. He asked what would be the feelings in this country, if an armed squadron were to be placed in the channel to stop and search our outward bound ships.

Earl Grey said, with regard to the United States, he agreed entirely in the opinion of acting in this matter with the greatest forbearance. However indignant he might be at the prostitution of the American flag in connection with slavery, "it was not only our duty, but true wisdom to the object that we had in view, to remain rigidly within our rights, and not by measures of questionable legality to put ourselves in the wrong." If he was not greatly mistaken, the order sent to our officers was not to interfere with *bonâ fide* American vessels, though engaged in the slave-trade.

The Earl of Aberdeen said that "the orders when drawn up had been communicated to and approved by the American government, and that the officers were acting under them, unless they had been recently changed, which he hoped had not been the case. They must have a reasonable suspicion that a vessel was not authorized to carry the flag she bore, before they ventured to visit her. A vessel might refuse to hoist any flag, and in that case all that they had to do was to see what she was. If she turned out to be a pirate, they might deal with her. If she turned out to be a Spanish vessel or the ship of any country with which we had a treaty, our officers might proceed accordingly; but if she was an American vessel or the vessel of any power with which we had no treaty, we could not interfere."

In the House of Commons, on the 18th, Mr. Bright, in putting a question to Mr. Fitzgerald, said that Lord Aberdeen had stated on the previous evening, that, according to the instructions of 1844, it was impossible that transactions, such as had been complained of, could have taken place. Now, he thought that it was highly improbable that British officers could have committed the acts alleged, unless they had received fresh instructions beyond those referred to by Lord Aberdeen.

Mr. Fitzgerald would now inform the Honorable gentleman what the views of her Majesty's government were as to the claim of the American government that the right of search or of visitation should be renounced. This right had no doubt been a constant source of irritation between the two nations, and, whatever might have been the practice of preceding governments of this country, it had never been admitted by the Americans. It had become the duty, then, of her Majesty's government, in consequence of the unfortunate circumstances which had recently transpired, to inquire what were our rights; whether, if we had such rights, we should be prepared to stand by them; and whether, if we had them not, we ought not at once candidly to disclaim them. They had accordingly taken the advice of the law-officers of the crown, whose decided opinion was that by international law we had no right of search, — no right of visitation whatever in time of peace. That being so, he need not say they had thought it would be unbecoming in the British government to delay for one moment the avowal of this conclusion. But while they perfectly acknowledged that England had no right to visit American vessels engaged in peaceful commerce, it would on the other hand be wrong to say that this country should abandon the policy which had so honorably distinguished her, or that she should cease to employ her fleets in putting down the slave-trade. On this point the position taken by the British government was exactly that which, in one of the most able state papers, had been laid down by General Cass in his letter to Lord Napier. In that document there was this passage: —

"A merchant vessel upon the high seas is protected by her national character. He who forcibly enters her does so upon his own responsibility. Undoubtedly, if a vessel assume a national character to which she is not entitled, and is sailing under false colors, she cannot be protected by this assumption of a nationality to which she has no claim. As the identity of a person must be determined by the officer bearing a process for his arrest, and determined at the risk of such officer, so must the national identity of a vessel be determined at the like hazard to him who, doubting the flag she displays, searches her to ascertain her true character. There no doubt may be circumstances which would go far to modify the complaints a nation would have a right to make for such a violation of its sovereignty. If the boarding officer had just grounds for suspicion, and deported himself with propriety in the performance of his task, doing no injury, and peaceably retiring when satisfied of his error, no nation would make such an act the subject of serious reclamation."

This, he believed, was strictly the position which we were entitled to take by international law. The American government had themselves acknowledged it on the face of General Cass's state paper to be that which "no nation would make the subject of serious reclamation;" and this course her Majesty's government would instruct our cruisers in future to pursue. The Honorable gentleman had also asked whether any addition had been made to our fleet in the Cuban waters. During the time that her Majesty's government had been in office, no such addition had taken place. And he might say further, that it had necessarily come under their consideration whether the continuance of our squadron in those waters was requisite for the object which we had in view, and whether there were not also attached to its continuance there objections of another and more serious character. It was obvious that the question of maintaining a squadron on the coast of Africa was very different from the question of maintaining one on the coast of Cuba. A squadron on the coast of Cuba was in the highway of American commerce. Each day it could not fail to meet numberless vessels of American origin peaceably engaged in trade. And it was obvious, that, as in carrying out the instructions given to them much must necessarily be left to the discretion of our officers, there must always be far greater risk of misunderstanding — if not collision — in the case of vessels in such a sea. Whereas on the coast of Africa, where the commerce was much more scattered, it was much easier to ascertain the character of a suspicious ship, than when she was among a number of other vessels pursuing lawful commerce. It was therefore now under the consideration of her Majesty's government whether it was not more desirable at once to withdraw our squadron from the Cuban waters.

Lord John Russell said: "With respect to the original instructions, they were issued by Lord Aberdeen after a great deal of consultation with persons fully competent to advise him, and among others, with Dr. Lushington. They were framed in the most temperate spirit, and after they were issued they were communicated to the government of the United States. During fifteen years those instructions had been acted on without any interruption to amicable relations. Now, the question arose whether the complaints that had been made had arisen from the increased vigilance — perhaps an overstepping of duty — on the part of commanders of British cruisers, or from the unwillingness of the Americans to submit to the execution of those instructions which, for fifteen years, they had seen practically carried out. And in either case, what was the duty of her Majesty's government? In the first case, their duty was to restrain the over zeal of our commanders, and it became us as a great nation to acknowledge and repair any wrong that had been done. If, on the other hand, the Americans were unwilling to see those instructions carried into effect, it would be for her Majesty's government to concert with the American government such measures as might be necessary in such a case."

The position which Lord Palmerston has occupied, and may occupy again, makes what fell from him a matter worthy to be noted.

Lord Palmerston said: "He quite concurred with the noble lord, the member from London, in thinking it was impossible to admit the naked principle, that the hoisting of the flag of any particular country was to be taken as an unequivocal proof that the vessel belonged to the country whose flag she hoisted. It was well known that every vessel carried, for signal purposes, the flags of various countries; and if the simple hoisting of the flag of England or the United States, or of any of the numerous South American States, were to be admitted as a complete and sufficient proof of the nationality of the vessel, piracy of every description would roam the seas with impunity, and every country possessing a mercantile navy would soon feel the disastrous consequences of such an admission. He had not understood the Honorable gentleman, the Under-Secretary, to have stated that the government had adopted that principle to the extent to which he had referred. He had been informed by his Right Honorable friend, the late First Lord of the Admiralty, that no instructions had been sent to the cruisers on the Cuban coast different from those instructions which were agreed on in 1844 in concert with the American government. He presumed that the fresh instructions which had now been sent out would be communicated to parliament, in order that they might judge in what degree the former instructions had been modified."

In the following remarks of the Chancellor of the Exchequer, Mr. D'Israeli, there might appear to be some reserve as to the extent of the concession to be inferred from what was stated by the Secretary of State in the House of Lords and by the Under-Secretary in the House of Commons, were it not for the explicit declarations understood to have been made to our government, and to which we shall presently refer.

"The Chancellor of the Exchequer might mention, that, without conceding the point to which the noble lord had just referred, and which they had not in any way conceded, her Majesty's government, after pointing out the terrible abuse of their flag, under the present system, and that piracy of the most flagrant character might be committed, had invited the government of the United States to favor them with their suggestions as to the mode by which such things might be prevented, and had offered to take those suggestions into consideration, and, if possible, to combine with that government in any arrangement that might promise a satisfactory solution of the difficulties which both governments at present experienced. They had not as yet received any answer to that proposition, but he was inclined to believe that it would be received by the government of the United States in the same spirit as it had been offered."

Treating the question, as the political advisers of the British crown properly did, as a subject of international law, they early referred it, as Sir Robert Peel and Lord Aberdeen ought to have done in 1841, to the examination of the law-officers of the government. And though in accordance with the general, though not invariable, practice adopted in England, the ministers have refrained from laying the opinions formally before parliament, the result as announced in their speeches accords with the communications made to Mr. Dallas in London, and through Lord Napier to the Secretary of State.

We have no reason to doubt the assurances which appeared in the *Washington Union*, that Lord Malmesbury promptly gave to Mr. Dallas, for transmission to Washington, a minute to the effect that "her Majesty's government recognize the principles of international law as laid down by General Cass in his note of the tenth of April, and that nothing in the Treaty of 1842 supersedes that law." And it is further understood, that Lord Napier has furnished to General Cass a copy of a despatch from Lord Malmesbury to the same effect, and which moreover declares that the doctrines of the secretary's letter are sustained by the authority of Lord Stowell and of the Duke of Wellington, and that England has utterly abandoned the assumed right, and thus closed the controversy.[1] Indeed, as affording a corroboration from an American official source, though not imparted in a formal communication, we may allude to the speech of Mr. Dallas to his countrymen assembled in London on the fourth of July. After noticing the difficulty that had occurred in the West Indies, he says: "Without referring to that question more closely, it is a point which is essentially connected with one of the fundamental principles of the American Revolution; that principle being the necessity of maintaining, on behalf of the great American people, as a great community, the independence of their flag. I am not now going to argue the question as to visit and search; but I should like, on the fourth of July, to announce to my fellow-countrymen that visit and search, in regard to American vessels on the high seas, in time of peace, is finally ended. While, gentlemen, I am enabled to announce this gratifying fact, I think it ought also to be accompanied by the assurance, that the termination of that for which we have struggled for nearly half a century has been brought about with a degree of honorable candor and fair dealing on the part of the British government which is worthy of every acknowledgment on our part."[2]

We have no disposition to question the sincerity of the British declaration; while we find, in the comments of the British and continental press as well as in the par-

---

[1] Washington Union, June 30, July 9 and 10, 1858.

[2] London Times.

liamentary discussions, a marked difference between the construction put on the present understanding between the two governments, and their former views of the attempt to waive the claim of visitation and search, through the provisions of the Ashburton Treaty. All seem convinced that a perseverance in the measures which, since the pretension of visitation as distinguished from search was set up by Lord Aberdeen in 1841, have governed the instructions sent to the British cruisers, would no longer be acquiesced in, and that unless a claim, wholly unwarranted by the law of nations, was abandoned, serious collisions between the two countries would ensue.

We are not aware that the action of the British government requires further sanction. The point in dispute has been yielded not as the concession of any existing right, but as the acknowledgment of what the law of nations now is, and ever has been. The English professedly give up nothing that they had a right to retain, — no privilege, the exercise of which was not of itself an acknowledged usurpation. The opinions of the law-officers of the crown do not make the law, but declare what the law always has been. The Earl of Malmesbury, indeed, in terms admits the correctness of Lord Stowell's judgment, rendered forty years ago, and which, however it may have been disregarded, is now received as a true and obligatory exposition of the law of the case. No treaty, no legislation, can add force to a recognized international right, nor in the face of these declarations can any subsequent ministry more readily resort to the ancient abuses than they could violate the provisions of a formal treaty. The case would be different as to us were we to yield in any form, however qualified, to a foreign nation a right which they do not now possess of visitation or verification of the nationality of our ships. That would be a cession of an incorporeal right which, equally with a grant of territory, would require the full sanction of the treaty-making power, which, under the Constitution, is vested in the President and Senate.

General Cass has already had the satisfaction of receiving from England, what he contended should, in 1842, have been exacted, as preliminary to all negotiations, a formal abandonment of the claim of visitation or search. Therefore, as regards any subsequent discussion of conflicting pretensions, the honor of the country is fully protected.

Our government, after the prompt manner in which England disavowed her claims, is in courtesy bound to listen to any suggestions that she may make; but we trust that we shall be exposed to no further complicated engagements as respects our maritime rights. Though not as a condition of renouncing visitation and search, yet as a substitute for their objectionable pretensions, England accompanied the recognition of our rights by a proposition for a conventional visitation, and in the latest parliamentary debates that have reached us, as well as in the preceding ones, the expectation is held forth that some arrangement of that nature may be effected.

The subject was alluded to by Mr. Fitzgerald on the 12th of July, in the discussion of a motion by Mr. Hutt to discontinue the practice of visiting and searching vessels under foreign flags, with a view of suppressing the traffic in slaves. He said, that the government, as soon as they found the right which they had claimed of verifying the flag of a vessel supposed to have slaves on board was one which they were not entitled to exercise, thought it becoming the dignity of a great nation to abandon it at once, at the same time they considered themselves at liberty, where there were grave suspicions, amounting almost to certainty that the American flag was not legitimately borne, to run the risk implied in ascertaining it. That very morning he had received a despatch from Lord Napier, who wrote, "General Cass stated to me that the course taken by her Majesty's government was worthy of a great and generous country. He assured me emphatically, that, after the satisfactory declaration that had been made by her Majesty's government, the government of the States would give their attentive consideration to any proposal which her Majesty's government might suggest for the verification of the nationality of vessels, and their right to the flag which they displayed."

On all sides of the house it was admitted that the detention of American vessels, without the consent of the United States, was wholly out of the question.

Though using the same language, we have been particularly unfortunate in framing treaties with England, in the construction of which both parties could agree. It was almost thirty years after the Treaty of Ghent, that the boundary line, as laid down in the Treaty of 1783, was definitively settled, and then it was effected by adopting a conventional line in the place of the one which, it is believed, was as clearly defined by a reference to natural objects as human language was capable of expressing it. The very Treaty of 1818 to regulate our rights to the fisheries under the Treaty of 1783, involved in an important question of public law, was itself the object of a new convention; while after calling on the Emperor of Russia to construe a passage, in the English language, affecting slaves carried off in the war of 1812, a second arbitration was only prevented by our receiving a sum in gross. Sufficient has appeared in the debates on the Ashburton Treaty to show how entirely the parties failed from the outset in coming to a mutual understanding as to its meaning. The very exchange of the ratifications of that most unfortunate arrangement, the Clayton Bulwer Treaty, opened the door for interminable negotiations.

As the law is now understood by both parties, the only matter connected with visitation or search, open for consideration, is to provide for cases of involuntary trespass. Dependent as each case must be on the attendant circumstances, which can no more be anticipated than the causes that would justify a political revolution, it is difficult to perceive how any definition of excusable trespass, that would be of any practical avail, can be established by convention. But it can hardly be supposed, that, if a convention is made, it would not embrace all analogous questions. And it is to be remembered that England is bound by the "declaration" of the congress of Paris, though Lord Derby contested its policy in parliament, to consider the four principles, which are the object of the declaration, as indivisible, and not to enter into any arrangement in regard to the application of maritime law, in time of war, which did not rest on them all. Among these rules is the abolition of privateering, which, even with the amendment proposed by Mr. Marcy, is of doubtful advantage to us, and which, nakedly, as now included in the declaration, would not receive the vote of a single senator.

Besides, though the minor powers, whose assent in any event is unimportant, are bound to England by treaty, no arrangement could well be made without the participation of France.

Any agreement which might be made with reference to ascertaining the nationality of a vessel at sea, even if carried out in good faith, would either be wholly nugatory, or would be open to all the objections arising from the maritime superiority of England, which have been opposed to her previous pretensions; and which can only be met by our changing our entire policy, and maintaining a navy equally large with that of Great Britain.

The French government, it was stated in the House of Lords, have proposed that a boat from a public ship should go along-side of a merchantman, but without the right to go on board unless invited. This evidently does not meet the British pretensions; and it is not very clear what good or what harm it could do. The boat may now, according to the decision of the Supreme Court of the United States in the case of The Marianna Flora, go along-side; but the merchantman is under no obligation to lie by or wait the approach of the ship of war.

Having got rid of the claim to enter by right, it is hoped that no conventional grant to invade our territory on the great ocean will be accorded. The view taken of old by the British government, in reference to impressment, should defeat any new arrangement for according search under any circumstances. Mr. Guizot, in the discussions on the Quintuple Treaty, remarked, that there was a distinction, on that account, between France and the United States. "The Americans," said he, "earnestly resist every right of visitation on the part of England, under whatsoever form it may be presented; and, in my opinion, they are right. If the English attempted to search for their sailors on board of French vessels, we should certainly resist them, as the Americans do."[1]

It is not improbable, that England, with the changes introduced in the manning of the navy, would now be disposed to yield for any verification of the flag in peace, that might give the semblance of a sanction to her ancient pretensions, the claim of impressing seamen from our ships, which, as the right of search for contraband remains, might, with as much reason as before, be practised, even if we became parties to the "Paris declaration." But, though we have ever been surprised that its renunciation, as well as the total disclaimer of the right of visitation and search, in peace, was not made by Mr. Webster a condition of acceding to the Ashburton Treaty, it may well be questioned whether we should now yield any thing for the abandonment of a usurpation which no power is hereafter likely to exercise towards the United States. Much less would we be inclined to subject our mercantile marine to a perpetual surveillance, to obtain an exemption from inconveniences, in any event, confined to the temporary and exceptional periods of war.

The interests of our country are undoubtedly safe with the responsible chiefs to whom our foreign affairs are primarily confided. No other citizens possess the same experience in regard to our European relations as the President and Secretary of State, and whatever

---

[1] Procès Verbaux de la Chambre des Députés, tom. 1, p. 81.

they might recommend ought to receive the most favorable consideration. But it is believed that no arrangement by which foreign ships can be permitted to detain our merchantmen on the high seas, in time of peace, can obtain the constitutional ratification of the Senate; and it is hoped that a conviction of that fact will prevent Lord Derby and Lord Malmesbury from pressing the subject further on the attention of our administration. For the interests of both countries, and as a means of avoiding future collisions, our maritime rights should be allowed to repose on the authority of the law of nations as now understood by England and America; and with the disavowal of the recent aggressions, and indemnity for such of our citizens as have suffered from them, we trust that there may be an end of all entangling alliances, in regard either to African slavery or inter-oceanic communications; and that the principles of Washington's Farewell Address may again prevail in the national councils.

Looking simply to our own interests, we of course require no further proceedings on the part of Great Britain for the recognition of our rights; but the best evidence that England can give in furtherance of her acknowledgment of the law of nations, as binding equally on her relations with the strong and the weak, would be the repeal of her statute of 1839, which has lost none of its objectionable features since they were so forcibly portrayed by the Duke of Wellington, and of that of 1845, which, though directed against a single power by name, is no less an assault on the independence of nations. It is true that an act of parliament can constitute no international obligation; still it affords the protection of his government to the officer acting under it. That it is not a mere *brutum fulmen*, the condemnation of Portuguese vessels formerly, and of Brazilian vessels more recently, avowedly for offences against merely the municipal law of England, is a sufficient evidence; while the United States have adequate ground of complaint in the mode in which the laws investing the officers of the British navy with a general police jurisdiction have been executed.

This brings us to a direct consideration of the expedi ency of terminating the obligations imposed by the eighth article of the Ashburton Treaty. The President's objections, when a member of the Senate, to that Convention, have been inserted in the appropriate place.[1] Those of General Cass, besides what might have been inferred from his opposition to the Quintuple Treaty, appear in a correspondence, commencing with a despatch from Paris to the Secretary of State, under date of the 3d of October, 1842, and which was protracted beyond his diplomatic service. To his argument, so well sustained by what immediately followed on the part of England, against any arrangement not preceded by a formal renunciation of her pretensions, allusion has already been made. He, also, forcibly referred to the provision for the African squadron. Departing, for reasons which would equally authorize interference in any other matter interesting to humanity, from our principle of avoiding European combinations upon subjects not American, it rendered it obligatory on us to place our municipal laws beyond the reach of Congress.[2] Nothing, of which we are aware, has since occurred to

---

[1] See p. 52, supra.

[2] 29 Cong. 1 Sess. Doc. Senate, Ex. Doc. Vol. VIII. No. 377

make that desirable which was then objectionable. On the contrary, however we may regard the palliative, Mr. Webster adopted the African squadron as a means of escaping from the alternative of either acknowledged submission to British pretensions or of forcible resistance. The voluntary acquiescence by England in the law of nations, as expounded by General Cass, leaves the sacrifices imposed by the convention wholly without a motive.

If, under other circumstances, any advantage could arise from the United States being a party to the blockade of the coast of Africa, a conclusive reason for the withdrawal of our squadron is now to be found not merely in the secondary position in which it stands to the English, but in the practical effect of the coöperation with the British cruisers and of the acts of parliament in question, to render abortive all attempts to punish our own citizens, engaged in a violation of our own laws. This was clearly foreseen by Mr. Buchanan in 1842, and is the necessary consequence of Great Britain's holding a power of attorney from all the secondary maritime States, as well as of her much more numerous fleet.[1]

It appears, from what has been heretofore stated, that, so far from there being an efficient understanding be-

---

[1] In 1854, the British had twenty-seven vessels, mounting three hundred guns; the United States four vessels, mounting eighty guns, being the number required by treaty. The fact of the omission of the provision, contained in the preceding treaties between England and France, fixing the proportionate force of the squadrons on the coast of Africa, was made, in the Chamber of Deputies, a serious objection to the Treaty of 1841. It was feared that England might thereby obtain a preponderance, but Mr. Guizot explained it as arising from the inability of the other powers to supply their quotas. Procès Verbaux de la Chambre des Députés, tom. 7, p. 68.

tween the British and American squadrons, a comprehensive system of compounding felony has for years been adopted on the part of British officers to protect, for their own pecuniary interest, Americans engaged in the slave-trade, if there be any such, from amenability to their own cruisers, by encouraging them to throw their papers overboard, and to be taken without any evidence of their nationality.

General Cass thus explains, in his note to Lord Napier, these transactions, which have been noticed on the authority of American naval officers. "The reason assigned for this procedure is said to be, that the punishment of this offence, by the laws of the United States, being death, persons found committing it under the American flag, if they cannot escape, prefer to be captured by British cruisers, with the chance of impunity, or, at any rate, of a less penalty than capital punishment. The crew is landed on the nearest part of the coast, while the vessel is sent to an admiralty court for condemnation, and *the proceeds, or a considerable portion of them, distributed as prize money, and an allowance made for each of the captured slaves;* and such slaves, it is understood, are transported under prescribed regulations defining their condition to the British tropical possessions in America."[1]

It was not from those, to whom sympathy with slave-dealers or slave owners could be imputed, that the most earnest movements for the withdrawal of our African squadron have proceeded. Mr. Clay presented, January 15, 1851, a petition from Rhode Island, signed by all the executive and judicial officers, the members of the two houses of the legislature, the faculty of the University,

[1] Mr. Cass to Lord Napier, April 10, 1858.

and many others, distinguished by their position and influence in the State. The memorial declared that the experiment had utterly failed, and proposed in its stead colonization in Africa as the only means of effecting an entire suppression of the slave-trade. The eminent statesman from Kentucky, in concluding his speech, said: "I doubt very much whether there would not be less loss of African life, if there were no attempt whatever to suppress the slave-trade by means of these squadrons, than there is in consequence of keeping them; the result of which is merely to multiply adventurers, to send out more ships, to run more chances, to take more risks, in order to secure the object of transporting the slaves to the Brazils or to Cuba from the coast of Africa. Sir, I believe there is no effectual remedy for the suppression of the slave-trade but the occupation in Africa of the coast itself, and stopping it at the threshold where it begins. By the eighth article of the Treaty of Washington we were only bound to continue that squadron for a period of five years. The five years have long since expired — in 1847; and yet we continue this squadron down to this time. Without reference to any of the subjects which I have thought proper to present to the Senate, without regard to the suppression of the slave-trade, without reference to the great interests of colonization, I think, as a mere measure of financial economy, it is worth considering whether we shall expose the lives of our gallant seamen in such an inhospitable climate, at such a vast expense, reaping so little benefit from the operation."[1]

As regards the subject of the memorial, it may be

[1] Cong. Globe, 1850–1, p. 246.

remarked that the condition of the free blacks, equally repudiated by the non-slaveholding and slaveholding States, is one which commends itself more to the sympathies of the philanthropist than that of any class which has a fixed and recognized *status* in our social organization. In most cases, at the South, expatriation has become the necessary concomitant of emancipation, while the constitutions of Indiana and of other Northwestern States contain express prohibitions against the admission into those States of free colored persons under any circumstances whatever; nor was such a provision deemed an objection to the constitution proposed for Kansas, by that political party which made the exclusion of slavery from the new States a fundamental principle. Everywhere they are placed under practical disabilities, and meet with no sympathy from the free white laborer. The contest now going on in Missouri for the abolition of slavery has no connection with their emancipation, the exclusion of free persons of color being a fundamental principle of the State constitution. It is discussed as an economical question; and the success of its advocates would lead not to the liberation of the slaves, but to their sale and removal elsewhere, where the climate renders more requisite the employment of that species of labor.

In our large cities of the North, colored men, if not by law, by a prejudice equally potent, are excluded from mechanical, and most other, except menial, employments. Even in Rhode Island, where the negroes have (in disregard of the construction which the Supreme Court of the United States have given the term) practically accorded to them, as included in the denomination of "native citizens of the United States," political privileges denied to naturalized citizens, the most marked social distinction is established by law. No person having the slightest particle of black blood can contract a legal marriage with a white, and even the minister attempting to solemnize such a marriage is subject to a penalty.[1]

If the old States of the North and East have abstained from the same legislation as the new free States, it may well be, because an extirpation more rapid than even that which attends the red man in contact with civilization has left among them few descendants of their former slaves; and were it not for the immigration of fugitives and free negroes from the South, in some of them the race would have already ceased to exist. Among the late proceedings of the Canadian Parliament was a proposition to impose a capitation tax on all persons of color emigrating there from any foreign country.

If it be feasible to give such an expansion to colonization as would admit of its being a refuge for those free negroes whom the policy of all the States excludes from incorporation with the white inhabitants, rendering their establishment a means of general amelioration to the African continent as proposed by the Rhode Island memorial, the expenditure for the abolition of the slave-trade might be made beneficially to affect interests common to all the States of the Union; and the twelve or thirteen millions wasted since 1842 on the African squadron would have laid the foundation of valuable colonies. To promote such an object, by making the descendants of Africans contribute to the civilization of their own continent, was the purpose for which the Colonization Society was es-

---

[1] Revised Statutes of Rhode Island, Ed. 1857, p. 312.

tablished in 1817, — the founders of which included some of the most eminent citizens of the South. It has not, however, been a scheme generally acceptable to those for whose special benefit it was undertaken. In 1850, the African-American population of the Republic of Liberia, which it founded on the coast of Africa, including the Maryland Colony, amounted to only 7,000; now supposed to be 10,000. There are upwards of 300,000 natives within its territory.[1]

In an article of this character, a subject itself susceptible of extended discussion, and presenting some points of debatable policy, cannot be adequately considered. With the effects of metropolitan legislation on the British and French colonies before them, we are not insensible of the jealousy naturally entertained of any suggestions from other sources, by those whose very existence, and that of their families, might be jeoparded by permitting the intervention of the federal government or of the non-slaveholding States in matters connected with their peculiar institutions. And however strong the argument in favor of African colonization, which the policy now prevailing in most of the States would seem to offer as the sole condition of practical freedom for the emancipated portion of the race, there are circumstances which present themselves in the course of this examination, well calculated to impair the confidence heretofore existing in the project.

In 1854, a resolution was offered in the Senate, when in secret session, by Mr. Slidell, of Louisiana, to abrogate the eighth article of the Treaty of 1842. The Committee on Foreign Relations reported in favor of the prop-

---

[1] Commercial Relations of the United States, Vol. I. p. 476.

osition, after stating, that, for the twelve years that we had then kept up a squadron at an annual cost of $800,000, the captures had only amounted to fourteen ships; and that Sir Charles Hotham, who had for many years commanded the British squadron, had declared the whole measure inefficient, and that the slave-trade depended entirely on the demand. In fact, the exportation of negroes had increased every year since the Ashburton Treaty went into operation. If the market of Cuba could be closed, there would be an end to the traffic.

On 26th of January, 1856,[1] the injunction of secrecy was removed from Mr. Slidell's resolution; but no further proceedings seem since to have taken place in reference to the subject. Nor does it appear that the withdrawal of the African squadron, in conformity with the provisions of the treaty, was proposed in connection with the discussion of the recent transactions in the Gulf of Mexico. But the propriety of abrogating the treaty has been referred to by Mr. Dallas, whose position affords him peculiar facilities for examining its practical operation. In speaking of the disavowal of the capture of The Panchita, as founded exclusively on the stipulations of the Treaty of 1842, in his note of October 9, 1857, to Mr. Cass, he says: "You will pardon me for suggesting, that, while this pretension of a right to supervise and reform the commercial pursuits of other countries, by the means of visit and search, is thus covertly maintained against the frank remonstrances of the government of the United States, it may be doubted whether it be con-

---

[1] Cong. Globe, 1 Sess. 34 Cong. 1855–6, p. 147; 34 Cong. 1 Sess. Senate Report, 195.

sistent with the national dignity to prolong the exceptionable compact, under whose express terms alone an immunity is recognized."

It was not contemplated by either Mr. Clay or Mr. Slidell (indeed, the latter expressly disavows any such intention), that the termination of the convention with England should affect the penalties against the slave-trade, nor could that be the case without further legislation. Yet it may be well questioned whether, for the object proposed, a punishment other than a capital one, which (considering the equivalent commerce now carried on by England and France in coolies and African "emigrants" under legal sanction) can scarcely meet the sentiment of mankind, might not be advantageously substituted. A milder penalty would, at all events, be more certain to be applied. Even in cases of murder, in several States of the Union, capital punishment is abolished.

In considering, in connection with another provision of the Ashburton Treaty, the encouragement now being given to the African slave-trade or its Asiatic substitute, and which, instead of being diminished, has been vastly augmented, by the mistaken philanthropy of England and France in regard to their West India and other colonial possessions, the very small practical result that the most ardent friend of the system can now hope to derive from the continuance of our squadron will be sufficiently apparent. But as the French treaty of 1845, and ours of 1842, have been usually placed in the same category, it may not be irrelevant here to notice, that, since the conventions of France with England have been allowed to expire, the semi-official organs of the former announce that "her reduced squadron on the coast of

Africa is only maintained to protect her commerce from the inquisition and annoyance of the English cruisers."

The negotiators of the treaty refer, in the ninth article, to shutting "all markets against the purchase of African negroes," as the only efficient mode of suppressing the traffic. Without now discussing the coolie trade inaugurated by England, nor referring to the limited supply of Africans for her colonies which the proceedings for the suppression of the slave-trade afford her, nor to the trade of Turkey and other Mahometan and Pagan countries in African negroes, as well as in Christian slaves from Circassia and Georgia, in 1842 the great slave-markets were Brazil and Cuba. The former no longer exists, not in consequence of the crusade against the slave-trade, but rather of its cessation. The true cause of the change is thus given by M. Pereira da Silva, in the *Revue des deux mondes:* "Not only the statesmen of Brazil condemn the trade, but all classes of the people. It is desirable that there should be no mistake as to the reason of this modification of public sentiment. It is not owing to the British government. While the English cruisers were endeavoring to stop the trade even in the Brazilian seas, it increased every day; their proceedings, under pretence of suppressing it, often injured the honest and legitimate interests of Brazilian citizens, and raised the just indignation of the country against England. The slavers took advantage of this feeling to enlist the sympathies of the inhabitants by making them believe that that power was only influenced by selfish motives, and that it wished to diminish the productions and riches of Brazil to the advantage of its colonies, whose products were similar. When, however, the imperial government made, in 1850, a frank and loyal appeal to the country, enlightening it upon its true interests, present and future, the Brazilians appreciated it, and gave to the measure a support, which becomes every day more and more secure. It is gratifying to be able to affirm that the trade is no longer possible in Brazil."[1]

As to Cuba, a consideration of the relations which have, with some exceptional periods, existed for a series of years between England and Spain, might have heretofore rendered it at least questionable whether the former power is sincere in its efforts to suppress the last of the old marts for African slaves, and with whose extinction all apologies offered for the maintenance of its maritime police would cease. Great Britain has treaties with Spain, which, if faithfully executed, would at least prevent the landing of any slaves in the West Indies; and if she did not choose to make the infraction of them a *casus belli*, no greater objection from its being a violation of the independent sovereignty of Spain could apply to her giving them effect through parliamentary enactments, than in the cases of Portugal and Brazil. Indeed, it has been understood that both Spain and England have regarded the continued protection of the latter to be essential to the maintenance of the existing authority of the former in Cuba; but in the proposition for the tripartite convention made to us by France and England, and which was so eloquently replied to by Mr. Everett, as Secretary of State, on the first of December, 1852, no consideration connected with the sup-

---

[1] Revue des deux mondes, 15 April, 1858, p. 832.

pression of the slave-trade entered.[1] On the contrary, when, during the preceding year, the presence of English and French squadrons in the Gulf of Mexico, on the alleged ground of preventing the landing of adventurers with hostile intent in Cuba, was complained of as constituting a sort of police over the seas, in our immediate vicinity, no justification was offered, based on any design to carry out an object of humanity in which the three nations were supposed to be equally interested, but the door was opened by new pretensions to a further exercise of maritime surveillance.

This subject has not altogether escaped the notice of those members of parliament whose opposition to the slave-trade was based on moral, and not political, grounds. It has been fully shown, that, as to Cuba, the whole system for the suppression of the slave-trade, even as regards those captured and condemned by the mixed tribunals, has entirely failed. If vessels are condemned at Havana, which, from the constitution of the court, seldom happens, and the slaves are declared free, inasmuch as by the convention the custody is committed to the State in whose dominions they are emancipated, they are handed over to slave-holders on the payment of certain fees, by which, it is said, the public charities of the island are sustained. From time to time their names are inserted in the registry in the place of the slaves who happen to die.

A suggestion, in 1854, from an independent member of parliament, that there should be no interference on the part of the British government to prevent Cuba

---

[1] 32 Cong. 2d Sess. Senate, Ex. Doc. No. 13.

passing to the United States, received a prompt response from a minister of the crown, showing that, at that time at least, opposition to our aggrandizement was paramount to the suppression of the slave-trade.[1]

A proposition to apply to Spain the same policy as had been adopted towards Portugal and Brazil, was opposed by Lord Palmerston for reasons which, supposing the British course in reference to the other cases defensible, would strengthen, rather than impair, the ground for intervention.[2] Brazil they coerced because they had no convention with her, while, from the mere fact of Spain having made a treaty, she was at liberty to violate its provisions, as well as all previous engagements, with impunity.

But it is not impossible, if England has renounced, without any *arrière pensée*, her maritime aspirations, that among the fruits of our recent diplomatic victory may be the consummation of an object, which, though never attempted to be attained, despite the many provocations that Spain has given us, by any attack on the legitimate rights of other nations, has long been deemed essential to the security of an important section of the Union, while its acquisition would, through the markets opened to the merchants and manufacturers of the North and East, contribute immeasurably to our general national prosperity.

It is also a happy circumstance as regards the general peace of the world, that there is at this conjuncture a ministry whose political history is not

---

[1] Hansard's Parliamentary Reports, Vol. CXXXII., p. 128.

[2] Hansard's Parliamentary Reports, Vol. CXLVI. p. 1492.

identified with a system, of which Lord Brougham, and the Bishop of Oxford, who inherits the principles, with the name, of Wilberforce, are now the exponents, and whom all the reminiscences of St. Domingo might not deter from an attempt, in which Lord Palmerston might have concurred, to Africanize Cuba, in preference to an effectual suppression of the slave-trade by its cession to the United States. "I must say," remarked Lord Malmesbury in the late debate on the British aggressions, "that the conduct of Spain towards us on this question has been marked by the greatest ingratitude. We have taken her part on several occasions against those whom she has suspected of designs adverse to her. It has always been the policy of England and of other European countries to support Spain, and defend her in the occupation of Cuba against hostile invasions, as well as to prevent any agreement by which she might be induced to part with it. But if Spain continues to show that utter want of principle and that utter and base ingratitude which she has displayed towards this country, which has always been her friend, I do not hesitate to say that she must expect that indifference will be exchanged for amity, and, instead of our taking her part, she must expect us to leave her to whatever consequences may ensue, whether proceeding from her present conduct or not."

On a subsequent occasion, in answer to a deputation that waited on him on the subject of the slave-trade, Lord Derby said, "with regard to Cuba, he agreed that more could be done by the Governor-General than by any external force; that every exertion had been, and was every day being made, to bring the Spanish government to good faith in this matter; and that he trusted that the result might be brought about without a resort to coercive measures."

The following, from the London Times of the 14th of July, is even more significant of what may be the eventual policy of England than the declaration of any ministry, whose constitutional tenure of office is necessarily ephemeral. We insert the paragraph, without thinking it requisite to notice the remark in reference to the abuse of our flag, the incorrectness of which, though ministers have not refrained from similar unwarranted assertions, will be apparent to any one who has attended to the course consistently pursued by the United States for the suppression of the slave-trade, under every phase: —

"All this time, if we really wish to stop the slave-trade, and are ready to sacrifice our national jealousies to that object, we have already hinted at a most effectual course. The United States are, unfortunately, not above allowing the irregular use of their flag in the slave-trade between Africa and Cuba. But they stand rather too high in the scale of nations, as well as in their own esteem, to permit a slave-trade into their own ports. *Cuba once annexed, the whole trade comes to an end, and not a port will remain open, where the slaver can land his wretched cargo. Spain has long since forfeited all absolute claim to our interposition in her behalf.* Indeed, by this time, we presume, she would rather not be assisted by us, be the cause good or bad. Are we then prepared to make this sacrifice of national feeling for the sake of that philanthropy which we are always preaching to the world at the point of the bayonet and the mouth of the cannon? We ask no reply; we only suggest, that, if England chooses to regard the slave-trade as the greatest of human crimes, and its extinction an object worth fleets, quarrels, and wars, then she may some day be called on to prove her sincerity by acquiescing in the only means to this end, however disagreeable. We only wish that Spain could be warned in time; but warning is not for Spain. Had she listened to warning, she might still have stood in the first class of nations. But, as far as Spain is concerned, we must bow to Lord Palmerston's authority. She only regards force. Unfortunately, with all our cruisers, we have not the same leverage upon her as that in the hands of our American cousins. We may vainly attempt to watch her ports and scrutinize her traffic; *once they step in, they will wipe out, not only the slave-trade, but Cuba itself, from the list of Spanish iniquities.*"

If England really desires that the traffic should cease, an effectual remedy would be found in her aiding the transfer of Cuba, where alone, despite of the treaty stipulations between her and Spain, importations now take place. In our hands, no one can doubt that the laws, which have not been violated for half a century in the States and Territories of the Union, would there be equally operative, while all apology for visitation and search would also be at an end.

Nor is it an unimportant consideration, so far as humanity is concerned, that the slave-trade in Chinese and coolies, which, as it has been carried on in British ships, is attended, even according to the official reports to parliament, with all the horrors that ever marked the African slave-trade, may likewise be arrested. And although measures have been adopted, at the present session of parliament, having for their object, by prohibiting the carrying of Chinese or coolies to foreign possessions in British ships, to monopolize for the English colonies the labor of the Asiatics; yet if that law should be effectual, it would not seriously interfere with the supply for Cuba. The *Revue des deux mondes* says that the trade is extensively carried on in French vessels; and in a late number of the New York Herald, under the date of Havana, July 23, 1858, there is announced the arrival of four cargoes of coolies, one under each of the following flags, — Chilian, Peruvian, Bremen, and Spanish. Total, alive, 1,245, of whom thirty-four were females. Died on the way, from natural causes or self-violence, 288.

The United States alone of the three great maritime powers have been consistent in the prohibition of the slave-trade, not only the trade nominally so called, but they have effectually guarded against all evasions. We will not recur to colonial times, when the acts of the local legislatures for its suppression received the royal veto; but though the action of Congress under the Federal Constitution was restrained till 1808 with regard to the then existing States, all the States had, through their own legislation, prohibited the slave-trade as early as 1798; nor was it reopened, except by one of them in a single instance, extending during a period of four years. And of the slaves thus imported from 1804 to 1808, more than one half were introduced on English account.[1]

The act of 1794, prohibiting the carrying of slaves to any foreign country, and which was only preceded by that of Denmark in 1792, to take effect in 1804, is the

---

[1] Annals of Congress, 1819–20, p. 116.

law on which the United States rest their claim of having been the pioneer in the abolition of the slave-trade, while, in 1798, 1802, and 1804, acts were passed by Congress within the scope of their constitutional powers, as was supposed at the time, to prevent the importation of slaves into the Mississippi and Louisiana territories, and to extend the rigor of the enactments of 1794 in respect to the foreign slave-trade. In 1807, which was the year that the first British statute was passed, the law to abolish totally the slave-trade, after the first of January, 1808, was enacted. The laws of 1818 and 1819, as well as the act of 1820, making the engaging in the slave-trade piracy, have been elsewhere referred to. Nor did these statutes afford an opportunity, while holding out to the world a nominal prohibition of what all had concurred in condemning as a traffic "repugnant to the principles of humanity and of universal morality," to continue the introduction of African slaves under another denomination. The whole policy of these laws has recently been examined by one of the Justices of the Supreme Court of the United States, as well as by the chief executive officer in whose department the subject came up for a decision. On both occasions, the evasion so long existing in the English colonies to repair the consequences of the forced emancipation of their slaves, and which is now being practised in those of France, was proved to be wholly repudiated by American legislation.

Judge Campbell fully shows that the terms of the Constitution and the corresponding language of the slave-trade acts apply to apprentices and all those over whose person there is a power of custody or control, no matter how limited the term may be, for the object of compulsory service or labor.[1]

In May last, an application was made to the collector of the customs at Charleston, South Carolina, for a clearance of a vessel "for the coast of Africa, for the purpose of taking on board African emigrants, in accordance," it was stated, "with the United States passenger laws, and returning with the same to a port of the United States." The unusual character of the proposed transaction induced a reference to the Secretary of the Treasury. Mr. Cobb, who is a citizen of Georgia, regarding it as a violation of the law, as well as an attempted evasion of the settled policy of the United States, shows that though the Acts of 1794 and 1800 were confined in their operation to slaves *eo nomine*, the Act of 1807, and all subsequent acts, are intended not only to prevent the introduction into the United States of slaves from Africa, but of any negro, mulatto, or person of color, whether introduced as a slave or to *be held to service or labor*. "Whether or not," says the secretary, "the wisdom of our fathers foresaw, at that early day, that efforts would be made under a pretended apprentice system to renew the slave-trade under another name, I cannot undertake to say; but the language of the law, which they have left to us on the statute-book, leaves no doubt of the fact, that they intended to provide in the most unequivocal manner against the increase of that class of population by immigration from Africa."[2]

Were it necessary to produce any proof that the sentiments of the American people on the subject of the

---

[1] Charge to the Grand Jury in the Circuit Court at New Orleans, National Intelligencer, June 25, 1858.

[2] Washington Union.

slave-trade are unchanged, it might be found in the resolution, passed by the House of Representatives of the United States, on motion of Mr. Orr, of South Carolina (the present Speaker), December 15, 1856. It declares "that it is inexpedient, unwise, and contrary to the settled policy of the United States, to repeal the laws prohibiting the African slave-trade." This resolution had only eight dissentients to 183 voting for it, and of those whose names are recorded against it, several declared that they voted "nay," because they considered the resolution uncalled for. Had it been a practical question, the vote would have been unanimous.[1]

Nor is this opposition to the slave-trade mere empty declamation, which costs nothing. It is due to the reputation of our country that it should be understood, that, while other nations, by whom we are constantly vilified, clamorous in professions of philanthropy, are meanly eluding those restrictions on which they base their claims to superior virtue, and are turning to their own profit usurpations on the sovereignty of feeble States, exercised for the ostensible interest of the African race, the United States, from considerations of humanity alone, are foregoing the indefinite increase of those productions for which they have a monopoly in the markets of the world. Nor is this a sacrifice restricted in its consequences to one section of the Union. Cotton, serving as the great article of international interchange, adds not less to the resources of the North and East than to those of the slaveholding States themselves.

The revival of the slave-trade, with all the horrors of the middle passage, would nowhere meet with greater

---

[1] Cong. Globe, 3d Sess. 34 Cong. p. 126.

opposition, on moral grounds, than at the South. It is not to be forgotten that it was to the votes of the navigating States of New Hampshire, Massachusetts, and Connecticut, against those of Delaware and Virginia, that the slave-trade was left open from 1800 to 1808;[1] while it was a southern member (Mr. Wright of Maryland), who, in 1823, proposed that "we agree to a qualified right of search."[2] But though the United States possess a population of African descent of three or four millions, educated and trained to agriculture, it is wholly insufficient to bring into cultivation those extensive regions, for whose products, only limited by the quantity of labor applied to them, the demand has always been more than commensurate with the supply. The South, however, desires no admixture with her native American laborers of imported savages, but awaits for new *exploitations* their natural increase, the rapidity of which is the best indication of the kind treatment accorded to the American slaves.

Indeed, in the ten years between 1840 and 1850, the slaves increased, without including those who passed into the class of free negroes, from 2,487,455 to 3,204,313, while the whites, including a foreign born population of 2,240,535, only advanced from 14,195,695 to 19,553,068; and the free colored population, which was, in 1840, 386,303, with all the aid of emancipation, was, in 1850, 434,495. In no part of the universe is the same number of Africans so well cared for as in the Southern States of this Union. They are, in the scale of humanity, as much above the condition of their ancestors and of the

[1] Hildreth's Hist. of the United States, Vol. III. p. 519.

[2] Benton's Abridged Debates, Vol. VII. p. 459.

present inhabitants of the benighted continent from whence they came, and of the coolies and emigrants of the British and French colonies, as they are below the standard of the cultivated white man. It is not our purpose to enter into ethnological discussions affecting distinction of races, nor to palliate the enormities that attended the original introduction of the negroes into this country. But, as cognate to our present inquiries, we would remark, that, if a state of things, which, however susceptible of amelioration, experience proves to be the system best adapted to promote the well-being of the two races now among us, if not the only arrangement under which they can continue to coexist, is left undisturbed, there need be no fear of any violation of the statutes against the slave-trade on the part of the American planters.

What at an early day most favorably distinguished the condition of slavery in the British North American colonies from that of the Spanish and Portuguese was, that, while with us the supply was in a great degree kept up by the natural increase of those originally imported, the African population elsewhere was recruited by the annual introduction of fresh slaves, the problem to be solved being, in what time they could be most profitably used up. Even in the English West Indies, before the emancipation, the slave population, amounting to 558,000 in 1818, was diminished in twelve years by 60,000, and without including the manumissions in the account.[1]

It may be true that vessels belonging to or manned by Americans are occasionally engaged in the foreign slave-

---

[1] Edinburgh Review, July, 1850, Art. VIII.

trade, but if that is the case, they are in nowise connected with the planting interests, or with the owners of existing slaves; and the fault is not with the United States, but with those who might control the market, as England could that of Cuba, where the Africans are sold. If cases occur of those engaged in the traffic escaping the penalty of our laws, their impunity, it has been explained, is caused by the course pursued by the British cruisers; and, if American built vessels are employed by foreigners in the trade, it is only after a forfeiture of their privileges as vessels of the United States. It would be difficult, were it possible, for the government to prevent the sale of merchantmen abroad. Nor is it understood how the fact of a slave ship, built in the United States but belonging to foreigners, implicates us in the traffic, more than the manufacture, at Birmingham, of articles required for the slave-trade, does England.

The negro emancipation of the British West Indies was brought about mainly by a sentiment, which had been incorporated into the minds of the people of England, as a part of their moral and religious creed; while the great mass of them, (however as a nation they might be affected by the prosperous or adverse condition of the colonies,) had individually no direct pecuniary interest to interfere with the gratification of their philanthropy. Nor, owing to the influence of the periodical press, is even the limited class who influence legislation insensible to popular impulse. The Duke of Wellington, in counselling delay, was not more heeded in 1833 than when he attempted in 1839 to arrest those measures,—the result of the same spirit, to which the violation of our flag, in disregard of the law of nations, is traceable.

The colonists, attracted by the immediate advantages which the distribution of £20,000,000 seemed to present, and relying on the long period during which, under another name, their relation with their slaves was expected to continue, did not make even that resistance, which their connection with the diversified interests of the mother country might otherwise have enabled them to offer. Neither is it to be understood that the ministry, in yielding to the clamors of the professed abolitionists, had no other object than humanity in view. England's command of the ocean, and her immense resources, despite of the numerical strength of the blacks, precluded any danger of a repetition in the colonies of the catastrophe of St. Domingo. But undue confidence had been placed in those economical speculations which induced the belief, in disregard of climate and of the mode in which the agriculture of those regions can alone be carried on, that even for tropical productions free labor might profitably be made to supersede that of slaves. The effect, which their movements were to have in stimulating the slave-trade of those countries that practically tolerated it, was therefore not considered.

As it was supposed that emancipation, once adopted in the West Indies would be made general throughout America, the British government did not reflect on the advantages that they were giving to rivals prudent enough not to attempt radical innovations. What were their expectations on this point is manifest from the course subsequently pursued as to Texas. Mr. Calhoun wrote, as Secretary of State, to Mr. King, minister, at

Paris, that it was the design of England to avail herself of the position of that country, as a neighboring republic looking to foreign support, in order to operate through it on the domestic institutions of the Southern States.[1] That impression would seem to have been fully justified by the extraordinary despatch of Lord Aberdeen, of the twenty-third of December, 1843, to Mr. Packenham, and, by his instruction, submitted to our government. Lord Aberdeen unequivocally avowed that "Great Britain desires, and is constantly exerting herself to procure, the general abolition of slavery throughout the world."[2] Had the designs of England succeeded, her expectation was, according to Mr. Calhoun, to have compensated her losses in the West Indies by that preponderance realized for her East Indian possessions, which was contemplated at the time of the meeting of the congress of Vienna.

Great Britain had declared the political propagandism of the French Republic to be the apology for initiating wars that lasted for a quarter of a century. Without discussing the attack on national independence involved in both cases, it would be much easier to make one system of government applicable to all countries than to establish uniform regulations, without regard to the character of the population or the nature of the climate, with reference to agricultural labor. Even in England, at this day, we have vestiges of the feudal tenures; and in many parts of France predial servitude did not cease till the end of the last century, while Russia is now discussing a change in her system of serfdom.

Had England succeeded in her proselytism, the fate

---

[1] Cong. Globe, Vol. XIV. p. 5, Mr. Calhoun to Mr. King, Aug. 12, 1844.
[2] Ibid. Vol. XIII. Part II. p. 481.

of the Southern States would more likely have been assimilated to that of St. Domingo than to the condition of the British West Indies; but in either event the ruin, of which she would have been the cause, would not have been limited to our own planters. The four millions of people in England depending on the manufacture of cotton would not have been satisfied to perish for the furtherance of anti-slavery abstractions; and if Lord Aberdeen had caused a war of races in the United States, the royal family and nobility of England would probably have reënacted the drama which inaugurated the first French revolution.

Though slavery was abolished in the British colonies in 1834, yet an intermediate relation was to exist between the slaves and their former masters, originally fixed at twelve and seven years respectively, for predial and non-predial slaves; but which was reduced to six and four years, so that the apprentice system did not finally terminate till the first of August, 1840.[1] Scarcely had it begun to operate, before it was discovered that the aggregate labor of the emancipated blacks bore no proportion to what it previously had been in a state of slavery. And, since the abolition has been effected, the question has constantly been how to supply the deficiency; while, to avoid offending the anti-slavery party, the use of the appropriate term to designate the true character of the new laborers has been sedulously avoided.

As early as March, 1837, an order in council was issued, giving the consent of the government to a law of the colonial authorities of British Guiana, for the impor-

---

[1] British Statutes at Large, Vol. LXXIII. p. 666.

tation of foreign laborers, though the introduction of any from Africa, or islands peopled by an African population, was prohibited. And in July of the same year, by another order in council, the deportation, on an extensive scale, of Hindoos, called "Hill Coolies,"[1] was sanctioned. This measure was the next year vehemently attacked by Lord Brougham, who, recognizing in it the slave-trade in another form, predicted that they were about to expose to that infernal traffic the whole Asiatic coast. But it was an indication of how little (notwithstanding the hold that slavery abolition had on the popular sentiment) had been effected beyond the substitution of one race to another, that Lord Melbourne, then Prime Minister, remarked, that "Lord Brougham's ardent imagination was an unsafe guide in such matters. Slavery must exist as long as men thought it their interest to use slave-labor; and passionate appeals to the feelings of mankind were not alone sufficient to insure its abolition."[2]

During the administration of the colonies by Lord Stanley (Earl of Derby), a general recruitment of Africans, of course to be considered nominally free, was only resisted by the minister on the ground that it was premature, and might excite the suspicions of the powers united with England in the suppression of the slave-trade; while Mr. Hume, July 27, 1846, proposed the suppression of the squadrons on the coast of Africa, which had been found so utterly inefficient in stopping the slave-trade, and the organization of a system of ransom, which might break down the traffic in the

---

[1] Coolie means any East Indian laborer, whether agricultural or domestic.

[2] Annual Register, 1838, p. 92.]

places where it was carried on. Sir Robert Peel sustained Mr. Hume, saying, "Give all the encouragement in your power to the immigration of laborers, and pay no attention to imputations which you know to be unfounded."[1]

It appears from a parliamentary statement, that there had been imported, previous to 1846, into Mauritius,—which had, at the period of emancipation, 28,000 slaves,—86,000 Africans, either taken from the slave ships, or introduced as free immigrants; into Jamaica, 11,500, of both classes; into Guiana, 40,000; and into Trinidad, 20,000.

In the session of 1848, the measures adopted to introduce laborers from the East Indies to Mauritius, and from the East Indies and Africa into the West Indies, being admitted not to have been successful, parliamentary guarantees were given to colonial loans to the amount of £660,000, for the purpose of meeting the expense of immigration. Lord John Russell, who, as Premier, had made the proposition, stated, that laborers might be brought from any British possession in Africa, "provided there was an officer on board the vessel who should take care that there were no transactions resembling the slave-trade, and that the person who emigrates to the West Indies should go there with his own consent." He also said, that "liberated Africans," from captured ships, were conveyed direct to the West Indies, instead of being sent to Sierra Leone.[2]

In a parliamentary return for 1849, it appeared that there had been 64,625 Africans emancipated in the

---

[1] Revue des deux mondes, 1er Janvier, 1858, p. 96.

[2] Annual Register, 1848, p. 11].

mixed courts at Sierra Leone since 1819; and during the preceding year in the vice-admiralty court, at that place, 5,282, all of whom had gone as virtual slaves to increase the labor in the British colonies.[1]

In 1850, the proposition of Mr. Hume, to which we have referred, and which was, like the French system, now so much discussed, to buy slaves in Africa, and send them as free immigrants or apprentices to the West Indies, was renewed in parliament. The retrogression both of the creole and negro population, in consequence of the emancipation act, was admitted; and it was declared that the latter, though they had, through the legislation of the mother country, gained an artificial command of the labor market, had fallen back far below where they had stood in the years of slavery. The black population, it was urged, was relapsing into barbarism; and it was again earnestly contended, that "the only means of relief consisted in the introduction of African laborers, the only class suited to the cultivation." [2]

General Cass, in his note to Lord Napier of the 10th of April (now become, by the reference to it by the government of England, as fixing the law of nations, a most important historical document), alludes to a statement, "by high authority, in the British House of Lords, on the 16th of March last, and not contradicted, that a law had been passed in the island of Jamaica, called a vagrant act, the real object of which was to reduce the free negroes in the island to slavery."

Later intelligence from that colony is given in an

---

[1] Parliamentary Papers, 1849.

[2] Annual Register, 1850, p. 52.]

extract from the Colonial Standard, a paper published at Kingston, of the 10th of July. It will throw further light on the nature of free labor, as understood in the British West Indies:—

"Notwithstanding the disallowance of the Immigration Act of the last session, we have still a thoroughly practicable immigration act on our statute-book, which, although confessedly less complete and less effective *in regard to the length of contract sanctioned by it in the first instance*, than the act which has been disallowed, is still quite equal to the effectual enforcement of every contract that might be concluded under it. Under these circumstances the Governor has resolved on immediately calling in the remaining moiety of the British guaranteed immigration loan of 1852, and on at once applying the amount to the importation of immigrants under the provisions of the Island Act of 1852, to which effect was given by Sir John Packington, while Colonial Secretary in that year. The Board, after a short consultation, unanimously agreed to his Excellency's recommendations as set forth in his minute, and authorized the appropriation of £20,000 for East India immigrants, and also a further sum of £20,000 for the introduction of Chinese laborers into this colony. The Board directed the balance of the £53,000, applicable to immigration purposes, to be appropriated to the introduction of African and other laborers.

"The Board also requested the Governor to intimate to the Secretary of State, that they were willing to pay £5 for each African immigrant forwarded to this island, as well as one dollar per head to the emigration agent at the port of embarkation."

The parliamentary papers show, that, between 1847

and 1856, there had been introduced into the West Indies 47,060 immigrants and liberated Africans, and into Mauritius, 97,542, of whom the greater part were from the East Indies. Of those conveyed to the other colonies, about one half were from the same regions.

These documents disclose the horrible sufferings attendant upon the transportation of the coolies. An official report, in speaking of the mortality on board of a British transportation ship, says, that of 500 embarked, only 202 were landed, and of another, that 110 died by natural death and suicide. "What," it adds, "if it turns out that these were cargoes of veritable slaves, captured or kidnapped in the Bay of Bengal or Bay of Hong Kong, instead of the Bight of Benin or the Mozambique Channel, and conveyed in British ships to the slave mart of Havana?"[1] Even under the most favorable circumstances the mortality in British ships is said to be from fourteen to fifteen per cent., and though in the case of shipments to the English colonies, better regulations may be observed, yet that is confessedly not the case as to those that are sent to Cuba.

The Earl of Carnarvon, in the debate of the 21st of June last, said: "It was obvious, that, even if the law was not evaded, as was generally the case with respect to vessels clearing out for foreign ports, the government had no authority over them when they reached their destination. With regard to British possessions the case was very different. Between the years 1834 and 1856 no fewer than 170,000 coolies had been conveyed to Mauritius; and in 1856 no fewer than 134,000 remained. In the years 1852–4 the number of Chinese

---

[1] Parliamentary Papers, Vol. X. 1857.

conveyed on board British ships to British possessions was 2,340, of whom there had died on the passage 230, or ten per cent.,—certainly a very large percentage. But in the ten years, 1847–57, 9,600 persons were conveyed on board twenty-six British ships to Cuba, and of these, 1,391 died, or nearly fourteen and a half per cent. He was afraid that what the Bishop of Oxford had stated with regard to kidnapping was quite true, and that those poor people were got on board not only by kidnapping, but by false pretences, by devices of various kinds, and even by force. There was no reason to believe that the contract which it was alleged was entered into with these people was kept. On the contrary, the only evidence was that they were subject to a species of servitude, which, under the name of free emigration, amounted practically to slavery. *It might be said that the coolie was free when he was landed in Cuba; but it was quite unreasonable to suppose that a man in a strange country, cut off from intercourse with his own countrymen, could under such circumstances preserve his freedom.*"

Lord Carnarvon also stated, on the authority of Sir John Bowring, that the "'free immigrants' who are obtained in China for transmission to Cuba are for the most part either drugged with opium until they are insensible, and then taken on board ship, or violently seized and carried off, or, in many instances, openly purchased in China. When they are thus got on board, they are forced to sign what is called an indenture of apprenticeship, by which they bind themselves to work for eight years for stipulated daily wages (not exceeding thirty cents a day), and while on the passage to some colony of which they know nothing,—not even the name,—they are obliged to suffer privations and misery of the most revolting nature." A case is cited where a number of these wretched coolies were huddled on board a ship, and fell sick before they put to sea; and it was considered too expensive to give them medical aid, so they were landed on the beach and abandoned, where many perished from starvation, and many others were devoured by wild dogs and pigs. From the 3d of June, 1847, to the 1st of September, 1856, the total number of coolies imported into Cuba, was 11,586. It is calculated that quite an equal number perished on the passage. In one instance, out of a cargo of two hundred coolies, 132 died during a passage of 149 days. In another, 122 died out of 175 during a passage of 171 days.

The English documents furnish us with evidence that the Chinese and coolie immigration is not, even under the most favorable circumstances, like our African population, a supply of labor which, when once adequately furnished, will sustain itself. The Governor of Guiana, in writing to Earl Grey, October 31, 1851, says: "The only drawback to Chinese immigration appears to be that which has so materially impeded the beneficial development of the experiment of introducing the natives of India into this colony,—the difficulty of procuring female emigrants. There is no class of persons in the colony for them, with whom to form matrimonial alliances." Again, on the 24th of July, 1853, he says that the captain of an immigrant ship told him that "he hoped hereafter to procure, at least, as large a proportion of women as is now done in the case of coolies, which, though insufficient to place them on the footing of an increasing population, would be ample to obviate objections on moral grounds."

The supply therefore can only be kept up by continual importations. And when it is considered that in the West Indies, where, after the slave-trade became unlawful, only young men were imported, and which is the system that now prevails as to Cuba, it was deemed profitable to "use up" the negro in eight years, what prospect can the apprentice or immigrant, who enlists for that time, have of surviving his servitude, or if he should, through a superior constitution, be an exception, what means can he possess of vindicating his freedom? Should he even be emancipated, what is to become of the remainder of his miserable existence?

Till 1846 the West Indies had the advantage of high protective duties against all slave-grown sugar, which were defended on grounds connected with their special condition, even by the most earnest advocates of free-trade. Such, however, had been the diminution of labor, that, as early as 1850, Mr. Hume computed the loss which had accrued from the forced emancipation at £100,000,000 or $500,000,000.

The necessities of the colonies produced no relaxation of Lord Brougham's zeal as to the African race. In moving, in July, 1857, an address to the Queen to put down the slave-trade, he said, that to import a limited number of Africans must lead to a revival of the trade; that free immigration and apprenticeship were nonsense; and that the advocates of those systems used precisely the same arguments as had been employed against the abolition of the trade. In Jamaica, the cry was for immigration. The wages there were from ninepence to one shilling a day. It is idle to suppose that a poor African will find his way back to freedom and to his country, after ten years' service; the encouragement of the emigration of negroes from the coast of Africa to the West Indies, by purchase or the liberation of slaves, has a direct tendency to promote the internal slave-trade of Africa.[1]

But, however earnestly Lord Brougham has continued to sustain the cause of the negroes, his views, with regard to the Asiatics, seem to have undergone a great change, since his denunciation of that new species of slave-trade twenty years ago. While, on every occasion, vehemently assailing the analogous proceedings of France for procuring African emigrants, his remarks, on the 25th of June last, were no longer directed against the traffic in coolies, but he desired to save the blacks by obtaining a monopoly of their labor for the British colonies. He objected to the exportation of coolies, by fraud, force, and every species of misconduct, to other countries, where there was no possibility of watching over their shipment, or the treatment they received in these foreign settlements. "The true remedy lay," he said, "in a narrow compass, and could be readily carried into effect. It was absolutely to prohibit the carrying of the coolies either from India or the coast of China to foreign settlements."

Even the Bishop of Oxford, on the same evening, denied indignantly that he was opposed to the importation of coolies into the English possessions. He asked, "whether the government would be willing to take upon themselves the responsibility of devising means by which the immediate evils of kidnapping might not only be checked, but also that the taint and suspicion of the slave-trade might not be brought on the lawful, hon-

---

[1] Hansard's Parl. Deb. N. S., Vol. CXLVI. p. 1661.

orable, and most desirable transmission of free coolies, who were willing to go, and who knew where they were going." [1]

A recollection of the horrible events, attendant upon a premature emancipation in Saint Domingo, might well have induced France to hesitate before entering on a repetition of a similar project for her remaining colonies. During the reign of Louis Phillippe, though strenuous efforts, which most sensibly affected the value of colonial property, were made to follow the example of England, they were always resisted by the government. The liberation of the negroes was one of the results of the revolution of February, 1848. It was decreed on the 27th of April, but it was not till the 30th of April of the ensuing year that an indemnity to the masters of 126,000,000 francs was voted.[2]

The immediate consequence of this legislation was, the falling off of the products in Gaudeloupe and Martinique, to the extent of one half as compared with 1847, and which diminution was greater in 1849 and 1850; while in Guiana and the Isle of Bourbon, or Réunion, the results were still more disastrous. "Now the question is," says an advocate of abolition, "how to find abroad, and introduce to the soil of the colonies, while respecting freedom, the amount of labor which emancipation has lost for them." Cuba had anticipated the French in the Chinese trade, though in 1856 a shipment was made from Shanghai to the French West Indies.

---

[1] London Times, June 26, 1858.

[2] The indemnity gave an average value in all the colonies, taken together, of 530 francs for each slave, and which differed, according to locality, from 705 francs 38 cents, to 430 francs 47 cents.—Revue des deux mondes, 1er Janv. 1858, p. 87.

Without government aid, there were, in March, 1857, 35,000 coolies in the Isle of Bourbon, who were as openly bought and sold as the African slaves formerly were; and a contract was made in 1853 for the introduction of 15,000 coolies into the West Indies, though, owing to the interference of the English government, it had not its full operation. The stipulated wages of a coolie is 12f. 50c. a month, besides food and clothing; and from 800 to 1,000 francs is paid for him to the importer.[1]

Bourbon has added to her East India laborers some Africans, recruited from the east side of that continent; while the government is carrying out a contract for the introduction of several thousand blacks into the West Indies and Guiana.

France has been induced, it is said, to adopt more extensive arrangements for the immigration of negroes, in consequence of the difficulties interposed to her obtaining a supply of coolies, whom she would have preferred. Although shipped from the French factories, they had been recruited within the British territory. She has, since 1852, declared to England, that "nothing, in the text of the treaties for the suppression of the slave-trade, prevented her taking the negroes that she might contract for on the coast of Africa, though they were ransomed, in order to be conveyed to the free and civilized soil of the French colonies; that if France had of late years abstained from resorting to this mode of recruitment, it was because she knew that it was repugnant to a respectable portion of the public opinion of England; but that, being under an obligation to secure

---

[1] Revue des deux mondes, 1er Janv., 1858, p. 87.

the success of free labor in her colonies, she would be obliged to renounce this friendly deference, if her ally continued to oppose obstacles to the free emigration of the East Indians."

In a debate in the House of Lords on this subject, on the 6th of July, 1857, Lord Malmesbury said that they must not consider getting laborers from the coast of Africa necessarily a revival of the slave-trade. "On the score both of policy and humanity, the question was worthy of the consideration of those who wished to take a broad and statesmanlike view of the subject. On the other side of the Atlantic, there were many millions of acres that could not be cultivated by white men; and if they were not cultivated by blacks, they must remain sterile; while millions of negroes, willing to labor, were confined to the coasts of Africa."

Lord Clarendon said that the French government had determined, in 1853, to purchase slaves in Africa, emancipate them immediately, and introduce them into the colonies. They would, they stated, make the experiment of free laborers.[1] On a subsequent day, July the 10th, in the Commons, Lord Palmerston said that "an attempt had been made to obtain free emigrants from the west coast of Africa for our West Indies. The attempt had failed. The negroes were not disposed to emigrate, and go across the sea; and there is, therefore, a great probability that the French government will be equally unsuccessful in obtaining really free emigrants; and that if the contract is carried into execution, it will be productive of a revival of all the evils of the slave-trade."[2]

---

[1] Hansard's Parl. Deb. N. S., Vol. CXLVI. p. 959. [2] Ibid. 1286.

To a deputation that came to Lord Clarendon in November, 1857, to complain of the French proceeding, he declared that it was an unmitigated and undisguised slave-trade. This statement he also repeated the ensuing month in parliament.

The announcement, made by Count Walewski to our minister in Paris, that "the British government would not object to the French scheme while the wants of the British colonies were being supplied by the coolie trade,"[1] produced no little sensation when repeated in parliament. The Emperor Napoleon is, however, not likely to recede from a measure, which is deemed essential even by those who most favored emancipation, for the restoration of the colonies to the prosperity which they enjoyed before 1848. Strong language has been used against it by the present English ministry, particularly in reference to a recent occurrence calculated to place the traffic in no very favorable light. Mr. Fitzgerald had, some time since, announced that a commission was to be appointed to treat with the French government on the subject, but, on a late occasion, he implied doubts as to that proposition being carried out.[2] He said, however, that he "believed that there was no power on the face of the globe that would make greater sacrifices to put down the slave-trade than the government of the Emperor of the French; but what was represented to the Imperial government was, that, although the free immigrants were most carefully attended to after they arrived in the French colonies, yet the system of buying African slaves on the African coast for the purpose of

---

[1] 35 Cong. 1 Sess. Senate, Ex. Doc. No. 49, p. 56.

[2] London Times, July 13.

apprenticing them for six years in a French colony, must necessarily lead to a continuance of the slave-trade."

Of the practical effects of the French proceedings, an experienced missionary in Africa thus speaks: "I suppose that for every slave landed in the American markets, about three persons are cut off in the wars and the famines which follow, and during the middle passage from coast to coast. The present system of apprenticeship affords a safer passage to America, but the apprentices are collected by the same system of destructive wars which have already depopulated some of the finest districts of Africa. No sooner was it known that apprentices would be bought, than the chiefs in different places began to make war on their weaker neighbors. My last advices from Africa told of famishing sieges and bloody battles to supply the French ships with emigrants."[1]

The case of The Regina Cœli has been specially noticed. She was a French emigrant ship which had on board two hundred and seventy "free emigrants," who, in April last, in the absence of the captain, took possession of the vessel and killed all the crew that were on board. She was subsequently surrendered to an English vessel and brought into Monrovia, when possession was regained by the French, the only question between the English and French being that of salvage. It was stated that there were manacles on board, and every thing to indicate the arrangements of an ordinary slaver.

Unfortunately for the colonization cause, by the French official accounts the government of Liberia would appear

---

[1] American Colonization Report, p. 39.

to be implicated in the transaction. It is said that not only had the President given it his approval, receiving a considerable sum ($1,565) under the name of passport money, for four hundred free laborers, with whom it was agreed the vessel should be supplied in forty days, but the enlistment had taken place under the superintendence of the Liberian authorities, as well as of the agent of the French government. The amount paid for these "free immigrants" was £2 10*s*. a head, as announced in parliament. It is conceded that they came from the territories of Liberia, but it is not intimated that they constituted any portion of the American emigrant population. They are said to have belonged to the Vey nation, who are within the jurisdiction of the republic, and it is understood that the purchase-money was received by their chiefs. These native tribes or nations enjoy the protection of the Liberian government, and are considered as in preparation for citizenship.[1]

The animadversions in parliament on the African emigation have induced retorts on the part of the French press. *The Constitutionnel* says "that it is demonstrable that France, far from engaging in the slave-trade, which it abhors as much as any other Christian and civilized nation, takes the slaves from the coast of Africa to make free laborers of them, while the English, on the coast of

---

[1] American Colonization Report, p. 54. From the statement of officers of the Colonization Society, it would seem that the government of Liberia is powerless to prevent foreigners from prosecuting their emigration schemes; though they had adopted measures requiring the emigrants to be brought to Monrovia to be examined as to their freewill in leaving, and passports were to be given to such as desired to emigrate. This may explain the payment under that head which is referred to in the text.

China, seize by violence or fraud freemen to make slaves of them.

"When an English cruiser captures a slaver, where does it take the cargo? Does it return it to the coast of Africa, and restore the negroes to their country and to liberty, or does it prefer to transport them to an English colony without their consent? These unfortunate beings, after being taken by force, or purchased on the coast of Africa, are sent to Demerara, Jamaica, &c., where they are obliged to contract an engagement to the queen for sixteen years, and are then distributed among the planters.

"We have received from London a calculation showing that the profits greatly exceed the expense of the fleets for the suppression of the slave-trade on the coasts of Africa and the West Indies. The prizes annually made by the cruisers exceed forty slavers, and, supposing only eighteen to be taken with human cargoes, the average being three hundred slaves for each vessel, England would have five thousand four hundred laborers, which she introduces into her colonies without asking their consent. Adding to these human cargoes the value of the merchandise and of the vessels and their outfits, as well as the money and other property belonging to the captain and crew, and we shall be brought to the conviction that the English fleet for the suppression of the slave-trade is not a ruinous work of philanthropy, but a very good business."

It may be recollected, as explanatory of the preceding article, that, of late years, by means of the legislation of 1839, the mixed commissions have had little or nothing to do, and that the condemnations have been in the vice-admiralty courts, and that thus the whole business of suppressing the slave-trade has been under the control of England, and all the captured slaves accrue to her benefit.

It is obvious, that, if we are to continue to make large annual expenditures, not for the purpose of executing our own laws and carrying out our own policy, but in the exercise of a general supervision over the morals of the world, Africa has no exclusive claims on our notice. To say nothing of the equivocal condition as to personal slavery among the millions subject to the sway of England in the East Indies, and which it is believed has been little practically affected by the nominal affranchisement of 1843, and the unheard of cruelties now being executed on others there, whose crime is a vindication of national independence, why should the slave-trade of Turkey be overlooked, especially the traffic in the Christian population of Georgia and Circassia, which is there superadded to that of negroes from Africa. England has more than once gone to war to maintain the integrity of the Ottoman Porte, and at this moment her efforts are being directed, by preventing their union, to retain the Danubian provinces, whose population is wholly Christian, permanently under the *suzeraineté* of the Sultan. The Bishop of Oxford, during the Crimean war, called the attention of the government to the fact, that the trade in Circassian slaves for the harems of Constantinople, which had been suppressed by Russia, had been reopened on the withdrawal of her fleet.[1] We do not perceive that when the Sultan was, by the congress of Paris, formally admitted to the advantages of the public law of Europe, he was even required to

[1] Hansard's Parliamentary Debates, N. S., Vol. CXXXV. p. 122.

subscribe to the declarations of preceding congresses in reference to the slave-trade, or to conform his domestic arrangements to those of Christendom; and it is, at all events, admitted that England acquiesces in his refusal to enter into any treaty for the abolition of the traffic in either of its branches.[1]

Conceiving that the relation in which England and France stand, with regard to a supply of labor for their colonies raising tropical products, is an essential matter connected with every project for the suppression of the slave-trade, on grounds of humanity, reference has been made, from the imperfect sources of information which were attainable, to such facts as may enable us to judge of the tendency of their present policy. Was it free labor as understood among us that was desired, the price of which is regulated by unfettered competition, it is obvious that there need have been no want of a supply from voluntary immigration. Since the disbandment of the West Indian laborers, Great Britain, especially has thought it necessary, on account of the excess of her own population, to encourage colonization to her North American and Australian possessions; and no inconsiderable portion of the labor of the States of this Union, where negro slavery does not exist, is performed by natives of the British isles, and that is the case also in the slave States as to all but predial labor. Indeed, at the same time that parliament was guaranteeing colonial loans for the introduction of African and Asiatic immigrants, it was voting money to facilitate the colonization of its redundant European population.

[1] Parliamentary Papers, 1856, Vol. LXII. p. 445.

That it is not free labor that is wanted, where the party can engage for as long or as short a time as he pleases, with the certainty of being able to enforce his contract, is therefore very clear. Between slavery, as it is understood by us, and the condition of the coolies and African immigrants in the West Indies, it is presumed that enough has incidentally appeared to show that there is no distinction which can operate to the advantage of the latter. Indeed, the very temporary nature of the engagement, if that is not altogether illusory, would be unfavorable to the nominal freeman. The life of the slave is valuable to his master, and, it is fair to presume, is therefore exposed as little as possible. All those employments that are most deleterious to human life are assigned to the laborers, from whose death the least loss would accrue. Nor can the experience of others be without benefit in guarding us against a repetition of their errors. To say nothing of patriotic considerations, or of fraternal regard for the whites; no friend of the negro race, who is made to understand that the injudicious emancipation in the West Indies is now the greatest obstacle to the final extinction of the slave-trade, can desire such a measure, however in accordance with his abstract opinions, to be applied to this country. The immediate effect of the abolition of slavery here would be the disorganization of the industrial system of the great producing States, attended with ruin to both existing races, and the derangement of the entire business of the whole civilized world, to be inevitably followed by a repetition of the horrors of the middle passage, and the other evils consequent upon a renewed importation of tropical laborers, — in other words, by the revival of the slave-trade in its worst forms.

The colonies neither of England or France exclusively supplied any commodity essential to the comfort and convenience of civilized man. The diminished production of sugar was compensated for by its increased culture, in countries not bold enough rashly to attempt experiments, that went to the subversion of the whole social fabric. But, for cotton, our Southern States possess a virtual monopoly. The quantity which they raise, varying from three to three millions and a half of bales, affords, with other slave products, an exportable annual value of from one hundred and fifty to two hundred millions of dollars. Our cotton furnishes the material for the most important manufactures of Europe and of our Northern States. In 1852, more than one half of the entire crop was exported to England, where it constituted three quarters of the whole consumption.[1] Notwithstanding the avowals in Lord Aberdeen's despatch of a general anti-slavery crusade, even during the most fanatical discussions in parliament, and when it was proposed to modify the general policy of free trade, by establishing differential duties for sugar, it was admitted that the exclusion could not be applied to slave-grown cotton, as the British manufacturers were dependent on the United States for that raw material.[2]

Powerful as have been the motives for England to keep up a system which, through her treaties with all the minor maritime States, enabled her to exercise a general police of the ocean, as well as to supply her plantations with captured slaves, there has been far from a unanimous sentiment in the British legislature for continuing an expediture deemed useless, for its professed

[1] Compendium of U. S. Census, p. 191.

[2] Annual Register, 1850, p. 521.

objects, by those whose experience had afforded them the best means of judging of its practical effects. In the sessions of 1848–49, the committees of the Lords and Commons came to opposite conclusions on the subject; and in 1850 a motion was made by Mr. Hutt for "an address to the crown, to direct that negotiations be forthwith entered into for the purpose of releasing [the] country from all treaty engagements with foreign States, for maintaining armed vessels on the coast of Africa, to suppress the traffic in slaves." This measure, there was reason to suppose, might have prevailed, had it not been for the determined opposition of the ministry, of which Lord John Russell was the Premier, and Lord Palmerston the Foreign Secretary, and who staked their political existence on the continuance of the policy. With all their efforts to defeat it, the measure obtained 154 votes against 232. In the course of this discussion, Mr. Gladstone, who had been Secretary for the Colonies, and was subsequently Chancellor of the Exchequer, said: "Although the burden cast upon the people of England by this charge was not limited to £700,000, that was not his main motive; he wanted to grapple with the question on the ground of humanity and philanthropy; and he had come to the conclusion, from evidence, of which he gave the details, that the present system of repression did not diminish, but, on the contrary, had a tendency to increase, the sum of human wretchedness."[1]

Nor do we consider that the little success which attended Mr. Hutt's motion, on the 12th of July, already noticed in another connection, for the discontinuance of the visitation and search of foreign vessels, affecting as

[1] Annual Register, 1850, p. 931.

it did the relations of England with foreign powers, indicated what the sense of the House might be respecting it, considered as a domestic question. Indeed, Mr. Cardwell observed, that it was not a motion to withdraw the African squadron, but to pass a resolution, and so fetter the hands of government; while the Times has given pretty unequivocal indications that public opinion was becoming adverse to a further continuance of the policy of forcible coercion.

The facts elicited in the last debate are not undeserving of notice, at a time when our own course, in reference to the suppression of the slave-trade, cannot fail to undergo examination.

The mover contended, that the experience of forty years had proved that an armed force could not put down the slave-trade; that, on the contrary, it extended and aggravated the evil; that the work was fatal to the gallant men engaged in the suppression service; and that England ran the risk of coming into collision with powerful States, thereby compromising the peace of the world; while all that could be said in favor of the present system was, that it had, in some inappreciable degree, checked the traffic. The slave-trade with Cuba, the parliamentary papers showed, was carried on with increased vigor, and almost with impunity, nor could any diminution be expected, without the concurrence of the local government. It would be, as it always had been, regulated by the principle of supply and demand. It was remarked by Mr. Burke, in his celebrated letter to Mr. Pitt, that the slave-trade could only be put down in the country of importation. He adduced the testimony of those connected with the Department of the Foreign Office charged with this subject, as well as of naval commanders, and of the Judge of the High Court of Admiralty, "that the squadron produced on the slave-trade little or no effect." That enlightened advocate of its abolition, Sir T. F. Buxton, had expressed his conviction before his death, that the slave-trade never will be put an end to by the course hitherto pursued. The Duke of Wellington had, as early as the congress of Verona in 1822, declared that the armed suppression system was a failure, and that the very attempt at suppression tended to the augmentation of the evil. The numbers put on board in each venture were so disproportionate to the capacity of the vessel, the mortality was frightful to a degree unknown since the attention of mankind was first called to the horrors of this traffic. The British squadron had not suppressed the trade, but they had increased its evils. If the coast was blockaded, slaves were kept in barracoons, chained together for weeks and months, dying of disease and privation, waiting an opportunity for embarkation. They were so packed on board ship that they were unable to change their position. The proportion that died during the passage was from twenty-five to thirty-three per cent.

In the remarks of the opponents of the resolution, great stress was laid on the squadron as operating on the fears of Brazil, and as a means of protecting British commerce in Africa, particularly in furnishing cotton, to compete with that from the United States; while even the introduction of Indians from Yucatan to Cuba was adduced by the First Lord of the Admiralty as a proof of success in arresting the slave-trade. On the other hand, it was confidently asserted, that, at the present moment, those who desired to import slaves from Africa to Cuba could get as many as they wanted; while, in order to evade the British squadron, a larger number were embarked, and the miseries of the trade greatly extended.

Lord Palmerston took the occasion to reiterate his objections to the repeal of the statute against Brazil.

Lord C. Paget, who had commanded on the African coast, gave a decided opinion against the efficiency of any squadron to arrest the trade. He said that nothing could exceed the aggravation of suffering, of which it was the cause, to the miserable beings. He once captured a vessel having 480 blacks on board, after a chase of seventeen hours, during which they were not allowed to move, and were kept without food and water. The proceedings of the British occasioned untold misery to the Africans, while they were utterly destructive of the health of their own officers and men.

Enough has been said to show, that, as far as regards the slave-trade, our position is not analogous to that of either England or France, for the double reason that our African population has not been emancipated, and that we are not now compelled to recommence the slave-trade, under another form, to restore our plantations to their normal condition. On this point General Cass well remarks, that "the United States have no tropical colonies reduced from a state of prosperity to adversity, and which they seek to redeem from this condition by the introduction of involuntary emigrants of any color whatever, for the purpose of carrying on the labors of agriculture. They have no necessity, nor any design, to resort to other countries for a supply of forced laborers, whether coolies or emigrants or apprentices, or by whatever name denominated, or of any laborers, who, if not compelled by actual force to enter into distant servitude, are compelled thereto by considerations little less voluntary, and in utter ignorance of the true condition into which they are about to enter."

It would seem, with the whole power of France, under a sovereign who brooks no opposition, directed to the protection of the trade for her colonies, while England neglects to act efficiently on Spain as to its suppression in Cuba, and is herself engaged in carrying on a more objectionable traffic in human labor, as well from Asia as from Africa, it would be absurd to attempt, with a squadron mounting eighty guns, to do any thing which could bear sensibly on the great result. It would be like closing a crevice in a rock, while the waters of the lakes were passing over the Niagara cataract. We abstain from what both of the great European powers are doing. We neither invite wars among the barbarous Africans for the capture of prisoners to be sold to us under the name of emigrants, nor do we entice or forcibly carry the unoffending Asiatics on board our vessels to be transported across the ocean to drag out a miserable existence devoid of all the domestic relations, and without that fostering protection which masters for their own interest, not to invoke any higher motives, are wont to accord to those in whom they have a permanent property. We do not covet the unfortunate wretches taken from the slavers of all nations, and whose fate by the capture is simply changed by having their destination altered from Cuba to Jamaica. On the contrary, our interposition in the cause of humanity, as far as it extends, is not only gratuitous in the expenditure of money and in the sacrifice of lives on the African coast, but, as early as March, 1819, effectual provision was made for the safe-keeping, support, and removal beyond the limits of the United States, of any Africans captured by our ships, and for the appointment of suitable agents on the coast of Africa to receive them.[1] It was this arrangement which efficiently contributed to the early success of the Colonization Society.

In conclusion, we would ask whether there exists any duty to the people or States of the Union, any international claims on us, or any benefit to accrue to humanity, even if it be competent for the federal government, from considerations of general philanthropy, to go beyond the functions distinctly prescribed for it by the Constitution, which would justify a continuance of the obligations imposed by the eighth article of the Ashburton Treaty.

The honor of the country requires that the gallant officers and seamen of the American navy should no longer act as purveyors of slaves for the British planters, and that our squadron should not be used as a tender to the British fleet, and as a decoy to bring within the reach of its cruisers the vessels of all nations, to be adjudicated on in the vice-admiralty courts of England. Moreover, as "the introduction of a slave into this country is a fact which the present generation has not witnessed," a just appreciation of the nature of our federal system forbids the application of the national resources to purposes in nowise connected with the enforcement of our laws; while a policy, coeval with our existence and never deviated from with impunity, condemns all entangling alliances with European powers.

---

[1] United States Statutes at Large, Vol. III. p. 533.

After the preceding sheets were in the press, the reports of further debates in the two houses reached the United States. As parliament was about adjourning, they are probably the last discussions of the session touching the subject, and are now introduced as necessary to a full history of the case.

In the House of Commons, on the 23d of July, Mr. Fitzgerald, to an inquiry respecting the intention of the government as to visiting ships suspected of being engaged in the slave-trade, replied, that the matter was under the consideration of government, but he could not be expected to state what course they would take under circumstances which had not yet occurred. He had, however, every hope and belief, from the language of the American government, and the American ambassador, that the matter would shortly arrive at a satisfactory conclusion.

Lord Palmerston considered this reply unsatisfactory. More information ought to be given. From what had been stated by the United States minister, he considered there had been some completed transactions. He therefore asked what pretensions had been given up, or what right conceded.

The Chancellor of the Exchequer (Mr. D'Israeli) is reported to have said, "there had been communications between the two governments respecting the alleged acts of British cruisers, and those communications were now in abeyance. During that abeyance the government of the United States had made a friendly overture that her Majesty's government should offer to the United States a plan for their consideration, which should accomplish all the objects that both governments had in view, namely, to put down the slave-trade without producing misunderstanding. Her Majesty's government had accepted that offer, and they were now engaged in the consideration of a plan, which they believed would satisfactorily accomplish all the objects that both parties desired."

No better explanation of these ministerial statements, as well as of those which had preceded them, can be given, than in the following language of the Washington Union of the sixth of August, which appeared before the last debate in the House of Lords was received in this country. It moreover shows why the ministers who have spoken in parliament have availed themselves of the remarks of the American Secretary of State and minister in London, attributable to diplomatic courtesy, for the purpose of holding out at home the idea of gaining, by conventional arrangement, what they have been compelled to abandon as a right.

"The claim of a right to visit our ships with a view to ascertain their national character has been fully and completely abandoned. This measure was adopted upon the opinion of the law-officers of the crown, announced in parliament, proclaimed in the public journals, discussed through England, and officially made known to our government.

"The British government, as we have stated, now ask our government to agree upon some plan by which our flag may be verified, and the anticipated abuses prevented. Lord Malmesbury evidently thinks, and rightly, that what the French propose—namely, suffering a boat to come along-side merely—will be of very little service. Should the United States agree to any plan upon this subject, that conventional arrangement will settle this point. But for ourselves we have very little confidence in such a result. If it does not take place, the parties will occupy their respective positions under the law of nations, that neither of them has the right to enter by force the vessels of the other under any circumstances whatever. If, after that, the immunity of a vessel is violated, it will be an act of trespass for which the government doing the injury will be responsible, and for which the government injured may require such redress as it thinks just; and this is all that can be said in any case of national injury.

"One remark may not be misapplied. The present British government have active, able, and experienced opponents watching them, and seeking at all times to convict them of errors and to remove them. The clear surrender of a long-cherished and long-enforced principle is a new fact in the history of the foreign intercourse of England. It provokes unfavorable animadversion, and is offensive to the national pride. The British ministry have to defend themselves in both houses of parliament, and desire, of course, to make the best of the case. Many things are said in the heat of debate which are merely one-sided, and give a very imperfect view of the matter. They are to be taken with many grains of allowance. The true position of England is to be tested by other and better considered proceedings, — by the written declarations of the cabinet. An instance illustrative of this is shown by Mr. D'Israeli's remark. He says, speaking of the action of the English and American governments, that there had been some communication between them respecting the alleged acts of British cruisers, and that the communications are now in abeyance (that is, under consideration, awaiting proofs) as to whether damages had been suffered, and to what amount, and that during such abeyance endeavors will be made to come to some agreement as to the visitation of vessels. All this is true, but it is far from being the whole truth. The remonstrance to the British government against this right of visitation contained in General Cass's letter to Lord Napier of April the 10th is not noticed here at all. That letter calls for no damages, but discusses a great principle. The demands for damages and redress were contained in subsequent letters, written after the forcible search of our vessels had taken place. But the demand for the abandonment of the principle is not alleged to be in abeyance, nor could it be, for it had been conceded, as Mr. D'Israeli well knew, and had thus passed from the category of national complaints, no longer in existence or abeyance."

The National Intelligencer, also published at the seat of government, says on the 7th of August: "We have had the satisfaction to learn that letters received from London by the last steamer announce the full and entire agreement, on the part of the British ministry, to the grounds assumed by our government in Secretary Cass's able despatch of the tenth of April last, and the consequent removal of all chance of misunderstanding growing out of diverse views on the subject hereafter. While our veteran and distinguished statesman may well be proud of the homage paid by the statesmen of England to the ability of his argument and the conclusiveness of his appeal to the principles of public law, the frank admissions made by Lord Malmesbury may be regarded as a fresh proof of the desire of the British government to avoid every just cause of irritation, and to cement the most friendly relations between the two countries."

In the House of Lords, on the 26th of July, Lord Lyndhurst, by whom it will be recollected that the phraseology of the Act of 1839 was materially modified,[1] asked for the correspondence with the United States, on the right of search question. He commenced by referring to a speech of Mr. Dallas's on the anniversary of American Independence, in which it had been declared that the right of visiting American vessels on the high seas was at an end. He said that some persons in high positions considered that the proceeding was not justified, and that a most important and valuable right had been sacrificed. "We have surrendered no right at all, for no such right as that contended for ever existed. We have abandoned the assumption of a right, and, in doing so, we have acted justly, prudently, and wisely. I think it is of great importance that this question should be distinctly and finally understood and settled. By no writer on international law has this right ever been asserted. There is no decision of any court of justice having jurisdiction to decide such questions in which that right has ever been admitted. I cannot refer to a better English authority than Lord Stowell. He says: 'I can find no authority that gives the right of interruption to the navigation of States in amity upon the high seas, excepting that which the rights of war give to both belligerents against neutrals.' Wheaton, the eminent American authority on international law, says: 'It is impossible to show a single passage of any institutional writer on public law, or a judgment of any court by which that law is administered, which will justify the exercise of such a right on the

[1] See p. 34, note, supra.

high seas in time of peace, independent of a special compact.' For myself, I have never been able to discover any principle of law or reason upon which such a right could rest. Lord Stowell further says, 'except by a belligerent power, no such right has ever been claimed, nor can it be exercised without the oppression of interrupting and harassing the real and lawful navigation of other countries; for the right of search, when it exists at all, is universal, and will extend to vessels of all countries.' In a well-known case, Judge Story expressed the same opinion.

"The rule in respect to the high seas is, that all nations are there equal. A merchant ship is part of the dominion of the country to which she belongs. What right has the ship of one nation to interfere with the ship of another when their rights are equal? No nation has a right to interfere with the navigation of another nation. Lord Stowell says: 'All nations being equal, all have an equal right to the uninterrupted use of unappropriated parts of the ocean for their navigation.' It may be that the flag of America is assumed by another power, to cover the basest purposes. That cannot alter the right. How can the conduct of a third power affect any right existing on the part of the United States? By a treaty with Spain, we have the right to visit and search Spanish vessels, for the suppression of the slave-trade. But that cannot affect the rights of America. If a cruiser ascertains, to the best of his judgment, that a vessel has no right to use the American flag, he may visit and examine her; and if his suspicions are correct, he may deal with her according to the relation of the country to which she belongs with England. America would have no right to interfere.

It would be a matter between the English cruiser and the vessel seized. If it should turn out to be American, we should apologize for the act, and make the most ample reparation for the injury. General Cass illustrates the point very clearly, by a reference to the case of an officer executing a warrant, who, if he is mistaken, and arrests a wrong person, must make ample compensation for the injury to the person arrested.

"A distinction is attempted, without any authority, between visitation and search. These are words that always go together in our international law, and are expressed in French by *droit de visite.* Mere visit does not give the necessary information. The moment you ask to examine the papers, or ask a single question, it is a search. The visit to a particular vessel, for the purpose of inquiry, is the exercise of a right comprehended in the *droit de visite.*

"Treaties have been entered into between different States, conferring the right of visit; but why make them if it is an international right? After the congress of Vienna, in 1815, France refused it to Lord Castlereagh. Richelieu said, 'France can never consent to a maritime police being established over her own subjects, except by persons belonging to her own country.' There is no such thing as the right of visit. We have renounced no right to the American government, for no right ever existed. It would be very material to adopt some plan by which a mutual understanding should exist that the integrity of the flags should be maintained. The question is, however, a difficult one. Her Majesty's government have acted wisely, prudently, and justly. It would be most unwise and imprudent to prosecute a claim that you cannot enforce consistently with law, or to attempt the enforcement of an assumed right, which may lead to resistance, and afterwards to war. No infliction can be worse to a nation than a war that is founded upon injustice."

The Earl of Malmesbury said: "I think the opinion of the noble and learned lord (Lord Lyndhurst) must be of immense consequence and value both in Europe and America. I feel that that opinion must finally settle the disputed point; and if ever a single question arises, that opinion must be quoted with his great weight, as he has quoted the authority of Lord Stowell. His views conform precisely to the opinion of the law-officers of the crown, whom we thought it our duty to consult before we answered the communications from the American government. They unanimously asserted that the international law, in reference to this question, was precisely as he has described it. Upon that opinion the government at once acted, and frankly declared that we had no legal claim to the right of visit and search, as hitherto assumed. We therefore abandoned both these claims, but at the same time put before the American government the paramount necessity of agreeing upon instructions to be placed in the hands of the naval officers of both countries, and, if possible, of all maritime nations, so that all acting in the same manner, commerce generally may no longer be obstructed, and at the same time the fraudulent use of the flags of foreign nations be prevented; at all events, such instructions as would save us from quarrels arising out of the assertion of an assumed right. The American government have stated to her Majesty's government that they are ready to listen to and consider any suggestions we may make to them, with the view to the verification of the flag. We have made the same suggestion to the government of France, who have appreciated the importance of the question. Although all agree that the dignity of our several nations would be more or less compromised by a right of search, I do not think there can be any doubt of the necessity of establishing some sort of security against the fraudulent use of the national flag. We have gone no further than this: we have abandoned the right of visit and search; and the American government have agreed to entertain and consider any suggestion we may make to obtain security against the fraudulent use of the flags of either nation. The French government are ready and anxious to assist us to attain the same ends."

The Earl of Aberdeen said that he had supposed the question settled in 1842 or 1843, when Mr. Webster declared to Lord Ashburton that the American government was satisfied. He does not understand what Lord Malmesbury means by saying that the question of the right of visit and of search had been referred to the law-officers. The instructions were drawn up under the inspection of Dr. Lushington and Sir G. Cockburn, and communicated to the American minister. The right of visit and search had been given up twenty years ago. He read from one of his notes of 1841 declaring that the British government renounced all pretensions to visit and search American vessels in time of peace, but that "it is the invariable practice of the British navy to ascertain by visit the real nationality of merchant vessels met with on the high seas, if there be good reason to apprehend their illegal character." Now, in ascertaining these facts, he had added, "the vessels referred to are visited, not as

American, but as British, or vessels of other states admitting the right of search."

The most ample reparation should be made for overhauling an American vessel suspected to be Spanish or a pirate. "I saw," he said, "some time ago an extract from a despatch from General Cass, in which that minister stated the case with the most perfect fairness, and almost exactly in the same words I have used over and over again." The most entire tranquillity for sixteen years was the result of his (Lord Aberdeen's) negotiations. The recent unfortunate affair had arisen from the zeal of cruisers transferred from the coast of Africa to the Cuban waters, and where they have converted into a rule that which was intended only as an exception. He did not apprehend how the right alluded to could be given up. Unless some mode should be adopted to verify the nationality of any vessel on the ocean, there can be no security for the preservation of the police of the ocean, so as to prevent the flag being assumed by all pirates. He was disposed to believe that if the "instructions" had been followed, they could not have occasioned dissatisfaction to any power. His last note remained more than a year unanswered, because the Secretary of State declared to the British plenipotentiary that the explanation was perfectly satisfactory. In it he had said that *the British government would maintain their right to ascertain the genuineness of any flag a suspected vessel may carry, and that to give up that right would be impossible.* "I think," he added, "that is the way in which, in common sense and justice, the question ought to stand and does stand at this moment. I was much pleased to see from his despatch, that General Cass has adopted the same opinion and used the same words as I myself employed. The exercise of this right, maintained as it has been for the last sixteen years, will not lead us into any bad position, even if no change is made in the instructions. If the noble earl can improve the system, I can have no objection."

Earl Granville never heard the law as laid down by Lord Aberdeen doubted. If any alteration was to be made it was important that Lord Malmesbury should state whether it was his intention to abide by the present instructions till the communications with the American government were concluded.

The Earl of Malmesbury said that Lord Aberdeen had omitted one very important point. He had assumed that the law was as laid down by Lord Lyndhurst, but he had not said that the American government went further, and contended that they alone had a right to maintain their own police, and whatever idea we had, if the American flag were flying on board of a vessel, we had no right to visit or to search her. They have consistently maintained that they would carry out their own police, and would be meddled with by no other country whatever. The difficulty is, the discretion that the officers should exercise. Lord Malmesbury is willing to admit that they were acting under their orders, but lately when the present government entered into office, there appeared to be a very much increased activity among their cruisers. In the exercise of the discretion which was given them by Lord Aberdeen's instructions, their officers certainly went to the extent of searching one American vessel, and they had no reason to suppose that they were acting improperly in so doing. The instructions have not been altered, though they might be improved so as not to expose the officers so much as they do to making mistakes. "Looking at the question in an international point of view, and pending the arrangement which I have sketched out that English cruisers should search suspected English vessels, that Americans should search suspected American vessels, and that French cruisers should search suspected French vessels, we have," he said, "without altering the instructions, suspended them until the negotiation proceeds further, and have issued orders to cruisers on that coast to respect the American flag under any circumstances. America, on her part, placed a considerable number of cruisers in those waters, and promised to use all possible endeavors to prevent her flag being used for the purposes of the slave-trade." [1]

This debate may well terminate the chapter on Visitation and Search in our diplomatic history. It leaves no room for doubt as to the abandonment of the British claim, while the difficulty of any conventional adjustment which does not concede to every country an exclusive police over its own vessels seems to be admitted. We repeat our conviction that none other can be made. Nor do we apprehend any inconvenience from the discontinuance by England of an usurped right. The law of nations is the same as it was before her claim was exercised, and, as has been noticed, a provision for search for piracy has never yet found a place in any treaty.

The powers which undertook to abolish privateering without the consent of the United States — the nation most interested in it — are again in conclave. With the exception of France and Turkey, they long since surrendered their flags to England, by the conclusion of

---

[1] London Times, July 27, 1858.

what was intended to be the Quintuple Treaty, or by otherwise according the right of search. It is possible that they may make some new law on this subject, which may obtain, as it is announced that the "Paris declaration" has, the assent of those mighty maritime States, Saxe Altenburg and Saxe Coburg-Gotha.

Lord Aberdeen only reiterated in his speech the English doctrines of 1841–2. He had again recourse to those verbal distinctions, by which he had assumed to have renounced, in his correspondence with Mr. Stevenson and Mr. Everett, the right of visitation and search of American vessels; while he continued to maintain as a right, a claim to the verification of the flag of every ship at sea, to be effected by the detention of the vessel, and the examination of her papers and "other proofs."

The Times, in commenting on the preceding debate, says: "Lord Aberdeen had stood out for so much questioning, stopping, and examining, equivalent to the actual stoppage and molestation of a suspected vessel, as would help us to discover whether the ship was American or not. This, his Lordship maintained, we had a right to do, and this he had stood out for. This he is prepared to demand; and the demand, his Lordship urges, is not at all incompatible with the total surrender of the right of visit and search. . . . . What other states demand, and what we have conceded, recently as it appears to us, is, that the smallest act of force or exhibition of superior strength, to the annoyance or interruption of a foreign ship on the open sea, is at once at our risk. We must do it on the speculation, that, if we turn out wrong in our suspicion, we must make proper apologies and reparation to the suspected party. *We have no right to fall back upon.*"

Another London journal, hitherto supposed to speak the sentiments of Lord Palmerston, reminds Lord Aberdeen that "the American government have always regarded the right of visitation and search, in reference, first, to the claim which England has made to impress British sailors from foreign vessels, a claim which led to the war of 1812; and secondly, in reference to the maritime police, which, by every means, England has endeavored to enforce for the meritorious object of suppressing the slave-trade. *Both questions were expressly left unsettled by the treaty of* 1842."

Again it says: "According to Lord Aberdeen's doctrine, because certain ruffians choose to make a fraudulent use of the American flag, British cruisers are to overhaul every American vessel which may be suspected to belong to a country with which England has an intervisitation and slave-trade suppression treaty. Even in Lord Aberdeen's last dispatch, it is declared that 'we maintain and exercise the right of ascertaining the genuineness of any flag that suspected vessels may carry.' The law-officers of the crown have now given a decided opinion, 'that, by international law, this country has no right of search, no right of visitation whatever, in time of peace.'" The Post adds: "There was a time when England could assert and enforce the highest and most exclusive maritime rights. By her own policy, she has for the future rendered all such attempts impossible. She might now as well seek to compel every foreign vessel in the four seas to strike the topmast as a mark of respect to the British flag, as to seek to enforce, in time of peace, rights which belong exclusively to a time of war."[1]

The statement by Lord Lyndhurst of the law as now acknowledged, and which concedes to us an exclusive police over the vessels under our flag, with the admission of Lord Malmesbury that the instructions of 1843, which vested in the naval officers a discretion that extended to the searching of the vessel require to be changed, will show how much has been gained by the late negotiations. The immunity of the flag is placed beyond cavil, in consequence of the course adopted by the United States; and though a total withdrawal of the existing instructions, with a repeal of obnoxious statutes, might have better accorded with a just regard for the rights of *all* nations, we do not think it possible that the order "to respect the American flag under any circumstances," will ever be withdrawn.

The sentiment of continental Europe is not less decided than that of the English press as to the extent of British concessions. To the *Revue des deux mondes*, which advocated the cause of emancipation, we have been repeatedly indebted for important facts. That journal, after vindicating the loyalty of the parties concerned in the affair of the Regina Cœli, and admitting that there was a delicate question for humanity in carrying out the contract system adopted by France on the coast of Africa, remarked, even in advance of the last discussions: —

"A vast change has taken place in the public opinion of England as to the means of suppressing the slave-trade. That police of the sea, which England had

---

[1] London Post, July 29, 1858.

usurped, that suppression by armed cruisers which Lord Palmerston especially had organized and maintained with an intermeddling obstinacy, that practice of search which not only had the inconvenience of costing her very dear, but of exciting, every instant, difficulties with the maritime powers, — that whole system is very near being abandoned as obsolete, and injurious to English interests, as well as inefficacious as regards the odious traffic which it was designed to destroy. More sensible ideas take the place of the system formerly espoused by Lord Palmerston. The English liberals understand that they are only deceiving themselves in attempting to impose by force their moral ideas on nations that will not adopt them. They recognize the principle, that every nation must follow its own views in matters of philanthropy, as well as regards political institutions ; and they no longer pretend to any other propagandism than that of example. The tory ministry and the radicals are agreed on this point, and the solution of the recent difficulties with the United States inaugurates this new policy. It was with the unanimous applause of the House of Commons that the Under-Secretary of State for Foreign Affairs, Mr. Fitzgerald, announced the views of the English government in reference to the American reclamations. The law-officers of the crown have declared that English vessels have not, in time of peace, the right of visiting vessels belonging to countries which have not granted them this right by a special treaty. Such is the position of the United States, and such is also ours with reference to England." [1]

---

[1] Revue des deux mondes, 1er Juillet, 1858.

For the eminent statesman, by whom our triumph has been achieved, it is a glorious consummation of that work, boldly undertaken on his own responsibility, the first fruit of which was the withdrawal of France from the Quintuple Alliance, and the defeat of the well-laid scheme of England for the attainment of universal dominion, under the guise of humanity. The juridical fame of Lord Lyndhurst, united with the judicial authority of Lord Stowell, now imparts a sanction to the doctrines of the American publicists, Cass and Wheaton, which no future minister of England can ever presume to question.

APPENDIX.

A. — See page 10.

ABOLITION OF PRIVATEERING.

(*Translated from the Paris Moniteur of July* 14, *for the New York Herald.*)

MEMORANDUM TO THE EMPEROR.

SIRE, — Your Majesty will deign to remember that the powers which signed the declaration of the 16th of April, 1856, pledged themselves to take steps to render the adoption thereof general. I have, therefore, hastened to communicate this declaration to all the governments which were not represented in the congress of Paris, inviting them in the mean time to accede to it; and I now have the honor to inform the Emperor of the favorable reception which the communication has met with.

Adopted and ratified by the plenipotentiaries of Austria, France, Great Britain, Russia, Prussia, Sardinia, and Turkey, the declaration of the 16th of April has received the full adhesion of the following powers: —

Baden,	Lubeck,
Bavaria,	Mecklenburg-Strelitz,
Belgium,	Mecklenburgh-Schwerin,
Bremen,	Nassau,
Brazil,	Oldenburg,
The Duchy of Brunswick,	Parma,
Chile,	The Netherlands,
The Argentine Confederation,	Peru,

The Germanic Confederation,	Portugal,
Denmark,	Saxony,
The Two Sicilies,	Saxe-Altenburg,
Ecuador,	Saxe-Coburg-Gotha,
The Roman States,	Saxe-Meiningen,
Greece,	Saxe-Weimar,
Guatemala,	Sweden,
Hayti,	Switzerland,
Hamburg,	Tuscany,
Hanover,	Wurtemburg.
The Two Hesses,	

The above-named governments acknowledge, then, with France and the other powers, signers of the treaty of Paris —

1. That privateering is and remains abolished.

2. That the neutral flag covers the cargo of the enemy, except when it is contraband of war.

3. That neutral goods, except contraband of war, are not seizable under the enemy's flag.

4. Finally, that blockades, to be obligatory, are to be effective — that is to say, maintained by a sufficient force to shut out the access of the enemy's ships and other vessels in reality.

The government of Uruguay has also given its entire assent to these four principles, except its ratification by the Legislature.

Spain, without acceding to the declaration of the 16th of April, on account of the first article concerning the abolition of privateering, has answered that she appropriated the three others as her own. Mexico has given the same answer.

The United States would also be ready to grant their adhesion, if it were added to the enunciation of the abolition of privateering that the private property of citizens, subjects of the belligerent powers, would be free from seizure at sea from the war navies respectively.

Save these exceptions, all the cabinets have adhered without reserve to the four principles constituting the declaration of the congress of Paris; and thus, in the international law of nearly all the States of Europe and America, a progress is declared to which the government of your Majesty, following one of the most honorable traditions of French policy, may congratulate itself to have powerfully contributed.

In order to authenticate these adhesions, I propose to the Emperor to authorize the insertion in the *Bulletin des Lois* of the official notes in which these adhesions are consigned; and if your Majesty agrees to that proposition, I will publish in the same manner the accessions which may reach me subsequently.

I am, with respect, Sire, of your Majesty the most obedient servant and true subject.

WALEWSKI.

Approved, NAPOLEON, the 12th June, 1858.

B.— See page 38.

Mr. Forsyth, Secretary of State, instructed, on the 12th of July, 1840, Mr. Stevenson, Minister of the United States in London, to address to Lord Palmerston an official note, of which the following is an extract:—

"If, in the treaties concluded between Great Britain and other powers, the latter have thought fit, for the attainment of a particular object, to surrender to British cruisers certain rights and authority not recognized by maritime law, their officers charged with the execution of those treaties must bear in mind that their operation cannot give a right to interfere in any manner with the flag of nations not parties to them. The United States not being such a party, vessels legally sailing under their flag can in no case be called upon to submit to the operation of said treaties; and it behooves their government to protect and sustain its citizens in every justifiable effort to resist all attempts to subject them to the rules therein established, or to any consequent deductions therefrom.

"The United States cannot look with indifference upon the laudable exertions made by Great Britain and her allies in the suppression of the slave-trade, towards the attainment of the great object in view; and, so long as those efforts are confined within their proper spheres, they will command applause and good wishes from the people and government of the United States. But they must be considered as exceeding their appropriate limits whenever they shall lead to such acts as those which form the subject of this communication. The President has been advised, that, on frequent occasions, the flag of the

United States, as well as those of other nations, has been fraudulently used by subjects of other countries to cover illicit commerce, and elude the pursuit of British and other cruisers employed in the suppression of the African slave-trade; and that a pretext has thereby been afforded for boarding, visiting, and interrupting vessels bearing the American flag. The several complaints to which the subject has given rise should convince her Majesty's government of the great abuse to which the practice is liable, and make it sensible of the propriety of its immediate discontinuance. It is a matter of regret, that this practice has not already been abandoned. The President, on hearing of the abuses which had grown out of it, and with a view to do away every cause for its longer continuance, having now directed the establishment of a naval force to cruise along those parts of the African coast which American vessels are in the habit of visiting in the pursuit of their lawful commerce, and where it is alleged that the slave-trade has been carried on under an illegal use of the flag of the United States, has a right to expect that positive instructions will be given to all her Majesty's officers to forbear from boarding or visiting vessels under the American flag. This expectation is now distinctly signified to her Majesty's government in the belief that it will see the propriety of confining the action of its agents to the vessels of nations with whom her Majesty's government has formed stipulations authorizing a departure from the rules prescribed by the public law, and thereby prevent the recurrence of circumstances inevitably productive of causes of irritation, and deeply endangering the good understanding now existing between the two nations, and which it is so much the interest of both to maintain uninterrupted." — 29 Cong., 1 Sess., Senate, Ex. Doc., No. 377, p. 27.

C. — See page 41.

Extract from a Despatch from Mr. Everett to Mr. Webster, dated Dec. 31, 1841.

Lord Aberdeen rejoined that Lord Ashburton would go with full powers to make a definitive arrangement on every point in discussion between the two countries. He was aware of the difficulty of some of them, particularly of what had incorrectly been called the right of search, which he deemed the most difficult of all; but he was willing to confide this and all other matters in controversy to Lord Ashburton's discretion. He added that they should have been quite willing to come to a general arrangement here, but they supposed I had not full powers for such a purpose.

This measure being determined upon, Lord Aberdeen said he presumed it would be hardly worth while for us to continue the correspondence here on matters in dispute between the governments. He of course was quite willing to consider and reply to any statement I might think proper to make on any subject; but, pending the negotiations that might take place at Washington, he supposed no benefit could result from a simultaneous discussion here. — 29 Cong., 1 Sess., Senate, Ex. Doc., No. 377, p. 89.

D. — See page 42.

At the opening of the session of the French Chambers, December, 1841, the King said: "Since the close of your last session, the questions which excited in the East our just solicitude, have reached their term. I have concluded with the Emperor of Austria, the Queen of Great Britain, the King of Prussia, the Emperor of Russia, and the Sultan, a convention, which consecrates the common intention of the powers to maintain the peace of Europe, and consolidate the repose of the Ottoman Empire." — Annual Register, 1842, p. [281.

The treaty referred to was that of July 13, 1841, for the closing of the Dardanelles; but though France was thus readmitted, as it were, to the great European Council of Nations, the effect of the treatment which she had received the previous year was not without its influence on the chambers, in reference to the Quintuple Treaty.

E. — See page 60.

In the debate on the 2d of March, 1843, on the bill for carrying into effect the treaty with Great Britain, a discussion involving the whole merits of the subject, as regards the African squadron, and the claim which gave rise to it, took place. Mr. Benton did not think that the treaty-making power had a right to dispose of the navy. If it had, it might bind the whole of it for an indefinite time, and for a purpose not political, but moral. He considered the stipulation for the African squadron a gross and fatal departure from the old established policy of the country. Besides entangling us in foreign alliances, it involved a vast expense of money.

Mr. Archer said that no specific provision was requisite in order to give the President the power of making an application of the sum necessary to carry the treaty into effect.

Mr. Calhoun said the treaty had not created the difficulty as to visitation, which had grown out of other circumstances. If war should take place we should be in a better position on account of the violation, by England, of express treaty stipulations. He believed that the President had put a true construction on the convention.

Mr. Rives, after stating that he was in favor of fully executing the treaty till there was some overt act of contravention on the part of Great Britain, said that he did not concur with Mr. Archer. He was of opinion that the stipulations of a treaty must depend, for their execution, on the free and responsible coöperation of the legislative department. He further said: —

"The message of the President to the House of Representatives, while denying the right of Great Britain to exercise a general police over the flags of independent nations, yet asserts that if the vessel of another nation — of the United States, for example — be suspected of piracy upon what shall seem probable cause, the seizure and detention of such a vessel by a British cruiser, though the suspicion turn out erroneous, would give rise to neither public responsibility nor any claim of indemnity to the owner. 'The *right*, under such circumstances,' says the message, 'not only to *visit* and detain, but to *search*, a ship, is a *perfect right*, and involves *neither responsibility nor indemnity*.' Now, Mr. President, I must say, with all respect, that this doctrine of the message seems to me not to have been very well considered, and cannot be easily reconciled with those impregnable principles of public law, upon which we have heretofore stood against the world in arms. I had supposed, that, if any principle of the maritime code had been triumphantly vindicated and upheld by the labor of American statesmen, it was this: that, in time of peace there is *no right*, in any case, on the part of a foreign cruiser, to interrupt or detain the vessels of another nation upon the high seas; that a vessel of a nation on the high seas, in time of peace, partakes of the inviolability of her territory, and that any entry on board such vessel, without consent, is, in the eye of the law, a trespass. If a vessel, under the circumstances supposed in the message, be suspected of being a pirate, a foreign cruiser may, upon her responsibility, stop and examine her; but she does so at her peril. If the suspected vessel be in reality a pirate, no harm will have been done; but if, on the other hand, she proves to be a *bonâ fide* vessel of the nation whose flag she bears, a trespass will have been committed, involving both responsibility and indemnity, according to the circumstances of the case.

"We admit, in the most unqualified manner, the right of British cruisers to visit, detain, and search their own vessels, Portuguese, Spanish, and Brazilian vessels, and piratical outlaws, even though any of them may have fraudulently assumed the colors of the United States. But, to render the act lawful, the vessels thus detained and searched must be truly what they are suspected to be, namely, British, Spanish, Portuguese, Brazilian, piratical, and not *bonâ fide* American vessels. It is an acknowledged maxim of universal law, that every party, while exercising his own rights, must take care not to *violate* the rights of others, *Sic utere tuo, ut non alienum lædas.*

"Our late able and distinguished minister in France (General Cass), who, at a critical moment for the honor and safety of his country, and with a promptitude and success which give him lasting claims upon the gratitude of the nation, came forward to vindicate the principles of our American doctrine in the eyes of Europe, and especially of our ancient and chivalrous ally, has furnished, in his admirable exposition on that occasion, an illustration of the subject, from the transactions of civil life, which cannot fail to carry conviction to every mind. He compares the situation of a British cruiser claiming, and acknowledged to possess, the right to visit and detain British, Portuguese, Spanish, and Brazilian vessels on the high seas, to that of a ministerial officer of justice under the municipal law who has a writ or warrant of apprehension against a particular individual. His lawful authority is to arrest A., but he suspects B. to be A. in disguise. This suspicion gives him no *right* to arrest B., but he may do so *at his risk.* If the person apprehended turns out to be A., the act is justified by the event; but if, on the other hand, he be truly B., then a trespass has been committed, and an action of false imprisonment lies against the officer. In this action, the damages, it is true, may be materially reduced and mitigated by the consideration of strong circumstances of suspicion in regard to the identity of B., and the little actual injury he may have sustained; but, in every case the inviolability of the personal liberty of the citizen is maintained and vindicated as an inexorable principle of the law. In like manner, we can never admit, as a matter of *right* (however circumstances in rare and extraordinary cases might be allowed to mitigate or extenuate the trespass), the claim of the British government to visit and detain American vessels on the high seas, in time of peace, because they may be suspected of being British, or other vessels lawfully subject to search, and seeking to screen themselves by hoisting American colors. If British cruisers, under such circumstances, visit and detain vessels which turn out to be *bonâ fide* American vessels, they do it, necessarily, at their risk, and without *right*." He elsewhere well says: "If British cruisers have the *right* to visit and detain all flags they meet on the ocean, to satisfy themselves by personal examination of their genuineness, they might enforce the right in case of any attempt to resist or evade it by the summary naval remedies of capture and confiscation. If a neutral vessel, in time of war, attempts to resist or escape from the exercise of the right of search, she, by that fact alone, subjects herself to capture and condemnation as lawful prize. The same consequence would analogically attend the *right* of visit, in time of peace, if it exists."

Mr. King, concurring with Mr. Rives, wished to learn from the chairman of the Committee on Foreign Relations, whether the portion of the President's message relating to the right of visitation, as regards suspected piracy, is correctly given in the printed copies of the message; and if so, what was the exact understanding of the principle.

Mr. Archer replied that he understood the law of nations to relate to piracy proper — not to the piracy of the slave-trade. — Congressional Globe, Vol. 12, p. 378, Appendix, p. 205.

The inquiry in question may be supposed to have been induced, not only by the message to the House of Representatives commented on by Mr. Rives, but by a preceding one of the 9th of January, addressed to the Senate, in answer to a resolution that called on the President, among other matters, for information as to the "danger there was that the laws and obligations of the United States, in relation to the slave-trade, would be 'executed by others,' if we did not remove the 'pretext and motive for violating our flag and executing our laws,' by entering into the stipulations contained in the 8th and 9th articles of the Ashburton Treaty." In that message the President, seemingly confounding statute piracy with piracy under the law of nations, had said: "Vessels of the United States found engaged in the African slave-trade are guilty of piracy under the acts of congress. It is difficult to say that such vessels can claim any interference of the government in their behalf, into whosoever hands they may happen to fall, any more than vessels that shall turn general pirates. Notorious African slave-traders cannot claim the protection of the American character, inasmuch as they are acting in direct violation of the laws of their country, and stand denounced by those laws as pirates. In case of the seizure of such a vessel by a foreign cruiser, and of her being brought into a port of the United States, what is to be done with her? Shall she be libelled, prosecuted, and condemned, as if arrested by a cruiser of the United States? If this is to be done, it is clear that the agency of the foreign power has been instrumental in executing the laws of the United States. Or, on the other hand, is the vessel, with all her offences flagrant upon her, to be released on account of the agency by which she was seized, discharged of all penalties, and left at liberty to renew her illegal and nefarious traffic?"

F. — See page 98.

President Buchanan says, in his annual message of December, 1857: —

"The outrage committed on our flag by the Spanish war-frigate Ferrolana on the high seas, off the coast of Cuba, in March, 1855, by firing into the American mail steamer El Dorado, and detaining and searching her, remains unacknowledged and unredressed."

G. — See page 127.

The following is an extract from the Rhode Island memorial, presented by Mr. Clay, on 15th January, 1851, to the United States Senate. It is the more freely referred to as the author of these sheets was not among the petitioners. The paper was signed by citizens without distinction of party, and was headed by the then governor, the Hon. Henry B. Anthony, now United States senator elect:—

"We would respectfully remind you that all attempts to suppress this diabolical traffic through force of arms has ever signally failed, and that the blockade of the slave-coast by the fleets of Great Britain, the United States, and France combined, at an expense of more than $100,000,000 and the sacrifice of many lives, has resulted in a great aggravation of the evil, instead of promoting its suppression.

"We would also respectfully state that we believe that the only effectual barriers that have ever been placed between the slave-dealer and his victims in Africa have been planted on her coasts, and those have been found in every instance competent to its suppression or control.

"We would again respectfully refer you to a fact, which has now become unquestionably established as such by the results of experience, that that part of the western coast of Africa which ever has been and is now frequented by slavers, cannot be colonized by whites, the climate being deadly to their constitution, though friendly to that of the colored man.

"And lastly, we would remind you that about one third part of this coast has been successfully colonized by colored people from the United States under the auspices of the American Colonization Society, through the outlay, as your memorialists believe, of less than one million of dollars, and that the colonists thus planted have effectually suppressed the slave-trade as far as their jurisdiction extends, which we believe to be in extent, as before stated, about one third of the whole slave-coast of western Africa.

"Believing, as we do, that the African slave-trade is not to be suppressed by any armed intervention, and that experience has proved that colonization of the slave-coast of Africa presents the only feasible scheme for the suppression of the traffic, we most earnestly beseech you to take into immediate consideration the propriety of establishing a line of government steamers or sailing packets, for the purpose of conveying, free of expense, such free colored persons as may avail themselves of such means to emigrate to Liberia, or to any part of the western coast of Africa that may be peaceably colonized by them; or that an annual appropriation be made by government, in money, in aid of the cause of African colonization, to the same amount that is now expended in supporting the squadron of armed cruisers, and the outlay of which has, up to the present day, tended greatly to aggravate, rather than to suppress, the most crying evil that has ever existed on earth." — Providence Journal, January 20, 1851.

H. — See page 137.

The following extract from an article in the Newport Advertiser of October 29, 1856, is inserted as giving a summary of the negotiations that have taken place with Spain, with particular reference to Cuba: —

"Premising that no American, as I feel assured, who looks to the benefits already accrued to us from the acquisition of Louisiana and of Florida, of Texas and of the provinces, including California, ceded by Mexico, and to the position of Cuba in reference to our own security, in more than one sense, can doubt the desirableness of its possession to the United States, if it can be obtained consistently with our international obligations; there will be no difficulty in showing that there is nothing in the joint despatch to the Secretary of State of Messrs. Buchanan, Mason, and Soulé, dated Aix-la-Chapelle, October 18, 1854, and referred to by our opponents as the Ostend Circular, which is not entirely consistent with public sentiment, and with the uniform course of our government for thirty-four years. In the introduction to the last edition of 'Wheaton's Elements of International Law,' p. clxxiv., published in 1855, and before Mr. Buchanan was the presidential candidate, the views which have prevailed, whether democrats or their opponents were at the head of our affairs, are thus summarily stated: —

"'The whole policy which, since Spain by the independence of her continental possessions has ceased to be an important American power, has governed the United States, with reference to Cuba, was fully disclosed in the papers communicated by President Fillmore to Congress, in July, 1852, and which comprise the correspondence on that subject, going back to 1822. At that period, England, not apprehending the embarrassments which, since the emancipation of the negroes in her own islands, the character of the population would occasion her, desired the possession of Cuba, to give her the command of the Gulf of Mexico; and it was particularly feared, that, should she take the side of Spain, in the war in which the latter was about to be engaged with France, the price of English interposition might be the cession to her of the two remaining islands of Cuba and Porto Rico. Our policy ever has been, that, while we were content that those islands should remain with Spain, and would infringe no obligations of good neighborhood to obtain them, otherwise than by her voluntary act, we would never allow them to pass into the hands of any great maritime power. Not only have England and France been constantly apprised that we would not consent to their occupation by either of them, but, in 1826, at the same time that it was officially announced to France, "that the United States could not see with indifference Porto Rico and Cuba pass from Spain into the possession of any other power," we effectually intervened with Mexico and Colombia to suspend an expedition which these republics were fitting out against them. The United States, however, even at that period, explicitly declared to Spain that they could enter into no engagement of guarantee, as such a course was utterly inconsistent with our standing rules of foreign policy. The most recent indications also of the views of the American government confirm the preceding statement, and show, that, while we deem the acquisition of Cuba of the highest importance, and would give more than a full equivalent to Spain for a transfer to us of its sovereignty, we will not, without a more imminent necessity than now exists, make her refusal to sell it to us a ground for taking forcible possession of it, as essential to the safety of the Union.'

"The limits of this note prevent the citation of official documents *in extenso*, but it is believed that the following extract contains all that is usually referred to as objectionable in the 'Ostend Circular.' After remarking that the United States had never acquired a foot of territory, not even after a successful war with Mexico, except by purchase or by the voluntary application of the people as in the case of Texas, the despatch — which it is to be remembered was not a manifesto, or a 'circular,' as it has been most improperly termed, but a communication from foreign ministers abroad to the head of the State Department at home, and which it rested with our own government to publish or not — thus proceeds: 'Our past history forbids that we should acquire the island of Cuba without the consent of Spain, unless justified by the great law of self-preservation. We must, in any event, preserve our own conscious rectitude, and our own self-respect. Whilst pursuing this course, we can afford to disregard the censures of the world, to which we have been so often and so unjustly exposed. After we shall have offered Spain a price for Cuba far beyond its present value, and this shall have been refused, it will then be time to consider the question, Does Cuba, in the possession of Spain, seriously endanger our internal peace, and the existence of our cherished Union? Should this question be answered in the affirmative, then by every law, human and divine, we shall be justified in wresting it from Spain, if we possess the power; and this upon the very same principle that would justify an individual in tearing down the burning house of his neighbor, if there were no other means of preventing the flames from destroying his own home. Under such circumstances, we ought neither to count the cost nor regard the odds which Spain might enlist against us. We forbear to enter into the question, whether the present condition of the island would justify such a measure. We should, however, be recreant to our duty, be unworthy of our gallant forefathers, and commit base treason against our posterity, should we permit Cuba to be Africanized, and become a second St. Domingo, with all its attendant horrors to the white race, and suffer the flames to extend to our own neighboring shores, seriously to endanger or actually to consume the fair fabric of our Union.'

"In what respect does this language differ from that constantly held in the instructions of our Secretaries of State, and in the despatches of former ministers abroad? Mr. Adams, writing in 1823, as Secretary of State under Mr. Monroe, says: 'The transfer of Cuba to Great Britain would be an event unpropitious to the interests of this Union. The question, both of our right and our power to prevent it, if necessary by force, already obtrudes itself upon our councils; and the administration is called upon, in the performances of its duties to the nation, at least to use all the means within its competency to guard against and forefend it.'

"Mr. Clay, Secretary of State, in 1826, says: 'If the war should continue between Spain and the new republics, and those islands should become the object and the theatre of it, their fortunes have such a connection with the prosperity of the United States, that they could not be indifferent spectators; and the possible contingencies of such a protracted war might bring upon the government of the United States duties and obligations, the performance of which, however painful it should be, they might not be at liberty to decline.' And again, Mr. Clay says: 'Great Britain is fully aware that the United States could not consent to her occupation of those islands under any contingencies whatever.'

"Mr. Gallatin writes from London, December, 1826, 'You will see by to-day's papers that Chateaubriand, in his speech to the House of Peers, said, "that England could not take Cuba, without making war on the United States, and that she knew it." This I had told him when he was minister, and included France in the declaration. You renewed the declaration in a more official form.'

"In 1837, Mr. Stevenson, minister at London, wrote: — 'I felt justified in saying frankly to his Lordship that it was impossible that the United States could acquiesce in the *transfer of Cuba from the dominion of Spain to any of the great maritime powers of Europe;* that of the right of the United States to interfere, in relation to these islands, I presumed there could be little doubt; that whilst the general rule of international law, which forbids the interference of one State in the affairs of another, was freely admitted, there were yet *exceptions to the rule, in relation to the laws of defence and self-preservation,* which all nations acknowledged, and that the present was precisely such a case; that in this view, and with a sincere desire to guard against possible difficulties, I deemed it proper to say what I had, and hoped his Lordship would receive it in the spirit in which it was offered.'

"Mr. Forsyth, in 1840, instructed Mr. Vail, at Madrid, 'Should you have reason to suspect any designs on the part of Spain to transfer voluntarily her title to the island, whether of ownership or possession, and whether permanent or temporary, to Great Britain or any other power, you will distinctly state that the United States will prevent it at all hazards, as they will any foreign military occupation, for any pretext whatever.'

"Mr. Webster, Secretary of State, in 1843, says: 'The Spanish government has long been in possession of the policy and wishes of this government in regard to Cuba, which have never changed, and has been repeatedly told that the United States never would permit the occupation of that island by British agents or forces, upon any pretext whatsoever.'

"Mr. Buchanan, instructing as Secretary of State, in 1848, under Mr. Polk, the minister to Madrid, expresses the same views as his predecessors had done, and as are contained in the despatch in question.

"'By direction of the President, I now call your attention to the present condition and future prospects of Cuba. The fate of this island must ever be deeply interesting to the people of the United States. We are content that it shall continue to be a colony of Spain. Whilst in her possession, we have nothing to apprehend. Besides, we are bound to her by the ties of ancient friendship, and we sincerely desire to render these perpetual.

"'But we can never consent that this island shall become a colony of any other European power. In the possession of Great Britain, or any strong naval power, it might prove ruinous both to our domestic and foreign commerce, and even endanger the union of the States. The highest and first duty of every independent nation is to provide for its own safety; and, acting upon this principle, we should be compelled to resist the acquisition of Cuba by any powerful maritime State, with all the means which Providence has placed at our command.'

"Mr. Everett, Secretary of State, in 1852, having in a despatch, which is a model of diplomatic eloquence, rejected all idea of a Tripartite treaty between France, England, and the United States, to guarantee Cuba to Spain, thus concludes his notes to the French and English ministers: —

"'No administration of this government, however strong in public confidence in other respects, could stand a day under the odium of having stipulated with the great powers of Europe, that in no future time, under no change of circumstances, by no amicable arrangement with Spain, by no act of lawful war (should that calamity unfortunately occur), by no consent of the inhabitants of the island, should they, like the possessions of Spain on the American continent, succeed in rendering themselves independent; in fine, by no overruling necessity of self-preservation should the United States ever make the acquisition of Cuba.'

"Mr. Marcy, adverting to the correspondence consequent on Mr. Everett's note, in his instructions to Mr. Buchanan, in July, 1853, says: 'For many reasons, the United States feel a deep interest in the destiny of Cuba. They will never consent to its transfer to either of the intervening nations, or to any other foreign State.'

"The Cincinnati platform in no otherwise refers to the acquisition of

Cuba than is implied by the resolution that 'the democratic party will expect of the next administration that every *proper* effort will be made to insure our ascendancy in the Gulf of Mexico.' And the committee of the convention who waited on Mr. Buchanan to announce his nomination, having expressed their conviction 'that our foreign affairs will be conducted with such wisdom and firmness as to assure the prosperity of the people at home, while the interests and honor of our country are wisely but inflexibly maintained in our intercourse with other nations,' he replied:—

"'In regard to our foreign policy, to which you have referred in your communication, it is quite impossible for any human foreknowledge to prescribe positive rules in advance, to regulate the conduct of a future administration in all the exigencies which may arise in our various and ever-changing relations with foreign powers. The federal government must of necessity exercise a sound discretion in dealing with international questions as they may occur; but this under the strict responsibility which the Executive must always feel to the people of the United States and the judgment of posterity. You will, therefore, excuse me for not entering into particulars, whilst I heartily concur with you in the general sentiment that our foreign affairs ought to be conducted with such firmness as to assure the prosperity of the people at home, whilst the interest and honor of our country are wisely but inflexibly maintained abroad. Our foreign policy ought ever to be based upon the principle of doing justice to all nations, and requiring justice from them in return; and from this principle I shall never depart.

"'Should I be placed in the Executive chair, I shall use my best exertions to cultivate peace and friendship with all nations, believing this to be our highest policy, as well as our most imperative duty; but, at the same time, I shall never forget, that, in case the necessity should arise, which I do not now apprehend, our national rights and national honor must be preserved at all hazards and at any sacrifice.'"

I.—See page 143.

The following instructions of Mr. Reed, minister of the United States in China, to the American consul at Macao, with regard to the coolie trade, appropriately connect themselves with the instructions of the Secretary of the Treasury to the collector of Charleston, in reference to African "emigrants." Taken together they show that the good faith of the United States most emphatically contrasts with the policy of England and France, who are evasively substituting a more objectionable slave-trade to that, the suppression of which Great Britain has so persistently made the apology for usurping the dominion of the sea with the monopoly of the commerce of Africa.

COOLIE TRADE.

Mr. Reed to Consul Rawle.

"LEGATION OF THE UNITED STATES,
MACAO, January 5, 1858.

"Sir, — Since the receipt of Mr. Marcy's letter of the 18th ultimo, written on your behalf, my attention has been again called to the subject of the shipment, in American vessels, of Chinese laborers, commonly known as coolies, especially to the Island of Cuba.

"Full consideration of the matter has satisfied me of the necessity of a resolute effort to arrest a traffic which, in its inevitable abuses, is repugnant to the instincts of humanity, in contravention of the laws of the Chinese government, and as clearly a violation of the well-settled policy of the government of the United States.

"My immediate predecessor, as you are aware, felt it his duty to condemn this trade by a proclamation, or circular, in the spirit of which I entirely sympathize. Mr. Marshall, in 1853, made it the subject of earnest remonstrance and of anxious correspondence with the government at home. Neither effort has been permanently successful in putting a stop to it, and, learning as I do that the trade is in full vigor, not only in some of the northern ports of China, but that American vessels are now loading here for Havana especially, I feel it incumbent on me to try by a still more precise effort to prevent it.

"How far the transfer of coolies from the Chinese territory to the Portuguese colony of Macao, and hence to an American vessel for transportation, is a violation of the laws of China and the treaty by the American shipper, it is not necessary now to decide.

"So far as the citizens and authorities of the United States are concerned, the question of duty and responsibility may be disposed of more easily and precisely.

"I am satisfied that the carrying of Chinese laborers — coolies — in American ships from any foreign ports to any port, foreign or domestic, there to be held to service, is prohibited by Acts of Congress, and exposes the master to a heavy penalty and the forfeiture of his vessel on its arrival in the United States, and this whether the laborers be taken to the United States or not.

"This being so, there can be no question as to the duty of the United States officers in China, and I now point it out to you.

"Understanding that there is an American vessel ('The Flora Temple'), commanded by an American master, now lying in the roads awaiting a cargo of coolies to be carried to Havana, I request you, on receipt of this letter, to address the Spanish colonial authorities at this port, either personally or in writing, informing them of the views of this trade entertained by me as the chief diplomatic representative of the United States in China, and that I consider it expressly prohibited by law. I have every reason to hope, from the friendly relations of the government of her most Catholic Majesty to the United States, and of the personal high character of Mr. Cañéte, the Spanish consul-general, that this intimation will be sufficient to prevent any continuance or official sanction on his part to an illegal, and, therefore, prohibited trade.

"I request you further to call the attention of the master of the vessel to his responsibility, and to say to him that if he, being an American citizen, or resident of the United States, shall take on board, receive, or transport from this port, or any port in China or its dependencies, any Chinese coolie or laborer, for the purpose of disposing of such person as a slave, or *to be held to service or labor* in the United States or *elsewhere*, he will expose himself, on his arrival in the United States, to a prosecution for a violation of the Act of Congress, with the penalty of fine and imprisonment and the forfeiture of his vessel.

"You will further inform him, that, in the event of a disregard of such a premonition, given in a spirit of entire friendliness and fairness, I shall feel it to be my duty to inform the government of the facts, and to recommend a prosecution for so clear and deliberate a violation of law. I have no reason to doubt that such a recommendation will at once be regarded.

"I desire you further to furnish me with such evidence in the form of consular certificate, and affidavit of some competent person, of the facts of the shipment in case it be persisted in. There will be abundant time for the authorities at home to anticipate the arrival of any such vessel in Cuba, and to procure complete evidence there, provided you communicate in season the fact of the departure hence.

"You will of course understand that these directions are not confined to any particular case, but are meant to regulate your official conduct with reference to the prohibited trade generally. Copies of these directions will be sent to the consuls at the other ports.

"I have to request that for the future enumeration be made of all coolies shipped in American vessels from this port and forwarded to this legation. I shall be glad to have a statement of such as have already gone."

J. — See page 149.

Lord Aberdeen to Mr. Packenham.

"FOREIGN OFFICE, December 25, 1843.

"Sir, — As much agitation appears to have prevailed of late in the United States relative to the designs which Great Britain is supposed to entertain with regard to the republic of Texas, her Majesty's government deem it expedient to take measures for stopping at once the misrepresentations which have been circulated, and the errors into which the government of the United States seems to have fallen on the subject of the policy of Great Britain with respect to Texas. That policy is clear and simple, and may be stated in a few words.

"Great Britain has recognized the independence of Texas, and, having done so, she is desirous of seeing that independence finally and formally established, and generally recognized, especially by Mexico. But this desire does not arise from any motive of ambition or self-interest, beyond that interest, at least, which attaches to the general extension of our commercial dealings with other countries.

"We are convinced that the recognition of Texas by Mexico must conduce to the benefit of both these countries; and, as we take an interest in the well-being of both, and in their steady advance in power and wealth, we have put ourselves forward in pressing the government of Mexico to acknowledge Texas as independent. But in thus acting we have no occult design, either with reference to any particular influence which we might seek to establish in Mexico or in Texas, or even with reference to the slavery which now exists, and which we desire to see abolished in Texas.

"With regard to the latter point, it must be, and is, well known, both to the United States and to the whole world, that Great Britain desires, and is constantly exerting herself to procure, the abolition of slavery throughout the world. But the means which she has adopted, and will continue to adopt, for this humane and virtuous purpose, are open and undisguised. She will do nothing secretly or underhand. She desires that her motives may be generally understood, and her acts seen by all.

"With regard to Texas, we avow that we wish to see slavery abolished there, as elsewhere, and we should rejoice if the recognition of that country by the Mexican government should be accompanied by an engagement on the part of Texas to abolish slavery eventually, and under proper conditions, throughout the republic. But although we earnestly desire, and feel it to be our duty to promote, such a consummation, we shall not interfere unduly, or with an improper assumption of authority, with either party, in order to secure the adoption of such a course. We shall counsel, but we shall not seek to compel, or unduly control, either party. So far as Great Britain is concerned, provided the other States act with equal forbearance, those governments will be fully at liberty to make their own unfettered arrangements with each other, both in regard to the abolition of slavery and to all other points.

"Great Britain, moreover, does not desire to establish in Texas, whether partially dependent on Mexico, or entirely independent (which latter alternative we consider in every respect preferable), any dominant influence. She only desires to share her influence equally with all other nations. Her objects are purely commercial, and she has no thought or intention of seeking to act, directly or indirectly, in a political sense, on the United States through Texas.

"The British government, as the United States well know, have never sought in any way to stir up disaffection or excitement of any kind in the slaveholding States of the American Union. Much as we should wish to see those States placed on the firm and solid footing which we conscientiously believe is to be attained by general freedom alone, we have never, in our treatment of them, made any difference between the slaveholding and the free States of the Union. All are, in our eyes, entitled, as component members of the Union, to equal political respect, favor, and forbearance, on our part. To that wise and just policy we shall continue to adhere, and the governments of the slaveholding States may be assured, that, although we shall not desist from those open and honest efforts which we have constantly made for procuring the abolition of slavery throughout the world, we shall neither openly nor secretly resort to any measures which can tend to disturb their internal tranquillity, or thereby to affect the prosperity of the American Union.

"You will communicate this despatch to the United States Secretary of State, and if he should desire it, you will leave a copy of it with him."

Mr. Calhoun to Mr. Packenham.

"DEPARTMENT OF STATE,
WASHINGTON, April 18, 1844.

"The undersigned, Secretary of State of the United States, has laid before the President the note of the Right Honorable Mr. Packenham, Envoy Extraordinary and Minister Plenipotentiary of her Britannic Majesty, addressed to this Department on the 26th of February last, together with the accompanying copy of a despatch of her Majesty's Principal Secretary of State for Foreign Affairs, to Mr. Packenham. In reply, the undersigned is directed by the President to inform the Right Honorable Mr. Packenham, that, while he regards with pleasure the disavowal of Lord Aberdeen of any intention on the part of her Majesty's government to 'resort to any measures, either openly or secretly, which can tend to disturb the internal tranquillity of the slaveholding States, and thereby affect the tranquillity of this Union,' he, at the same time, regards with deep concern the avowal, for the first time, made to this government, 'that Great Britain desires, and is constantly exerting herself, to procure the general abolition of slavery throughout the world.'

"So long as Great Britain confined her policy to the abolition of slavery in her own possessions and colonies, no other country had a right to complain. It belonged to her exclusively to determine, according to her own views of policy, whether it should be done or not. But when she goes beyond, and avows it as her settled policy, and the object of her constant exertions, to abolish it throughout the world, she makes it the duty of all other countries, whose safety or prosperity may be endangered by her policy, to adopt such measures as they may deem necessary for their protection.

"It is with still deeper concern the President regards the avowal of Lord Aberdeen of the desire of Great Britain to see slavery abolished in Texas; and, as he infers, is endeavoring, through her diplomacy, to accomplish it, by making the abolition of slavery one of the conditions on which Mexico should acknowledge her independence. It has confirmed his previous impressions as to the policy of Great Britain in reference to Texas, and made it his duty to examine with much care and solicitude what would be its effects on the *prosperity* and *safety* of the United States *should* she succeed in her endeavors. The investigation has resulted in the settled conviction that it would be difficult for Texas, in her actual condition, to resist what she desires, without supposing the influence and exertions of Great Britain would be extended beyond the limits assigned by Lord Aberdeen, and that, *if* Texas could not resist the consummation of the object of her desire, would endanger the *safety* and *prosperity* of the Union. Under this conviction, it is felt to be the imperious duty of the federal government, the common representative and protector of the States of the Union, to adopt, in self-defence, the most effectual measures to defeat it." — Cong. Globe, Vol. XII. part 2, p. 481.

K. — See page 150.

The great diminution in the trade between the United States and the British West India islands is also an illustration of the consequences of the abolition policy. No subject connected with our commercial intercourse had attracted more attention, from the time of the Revolution till the period of emancipation, than this trade, which was often sought for by us as a boon. So much importance was attached to it in 1794, that Mr. Jay introduced a provision into the treaty of that year, by which the United States, in return for being allowed to participate in it to a limited degree, were to be restricted from exporting all colonial productions, not only from the West Indies, but from the United States, to any other part of the world. Among the enumerated productions was cotton, of the existence of which, in our Southern States, the American negotiator was ignorant. (United States Statutes at Large, Vol. VIII. p. 123.) But though the operation of that article was suspended, and never went into effect, England, in 1815 and 1818, refused to include the West Indies and the British possessions in North America in the rule of reciprocity, as regards the navigation of the two countries, adopted for her dominions in Europe. (Ibid. pp. 228, 249.) The trade was repeatedly interrupted by retaliatory legislation. This was especially the case in 1826, in consequence of the United States omitting to avail themselves of the proffer, made by the act of parliament of July, 1825, to all nations not having colonies, to put the trade of Great Britain and her possessions abroad on the footing of the most favored nation. To remove these difficulties was one of the objects of Mr. Gallatin's mission in 1826–7, but in that respect he was unsuccessful. The interruption of this intercourse was used with effect during the Presidential canvass of 1828, and on the election of General Jackson negotiations were undertaken, which resulted in an agreement, by which the trade was resumed in 1830 under the legislation of the two countries. (American Annual Register, 1826–7, p. 22; Ibid. 1827–8–9, p. 4; Ibid. 1829–30, p. 52.)

But although all actual restrictions on colonial intercourse have ceased since the Act of the 12 and 13 Vict. c. 29 (26 June, 1849), and it is open to the navigation of all countries on the same terms as to the British, the imports from the West Indies into the United States, which, in 1795, were $6,426,091, in 1856–7 were only $2,653,698. Our imports from the Spanish West Indies, at the former period, were $1,739,138, and at the latter, from Cuba alone, $45,243,101. The total imports of the United States, at the same time, advanced from $69,756,258 to $360,890,140.

L. — See page 170.

New England consumed in 1856, 652,739 bales of cotton, or, at 450 pounds a bale, 293,732,550 pounds, costing more than $31,000,000, and the value of which was, when manufactured, at least $150,000,000. We learn from Mr. Claiborne's late report, that of 187,851,768 pounds imported into France in 1856, 175,613,672 pounds were from the United States. He also states that nine tenths of the consumption of cotton-wool in Switzerland was of the growth of the United States.

Of the importations into Bremen, the same year, of 45,539,585 pounds, 42,891,075 were direct from this country, and of the remainder, 1,790,107 were from Great Britain, a large portion of which was American. Into Hamburg in 1855 the cotton-wool imported was 48,083,451 pounds, of which 6,530,093 were imported direct from the United States, and 33,915,333, principally American, through Liverpool. In the States of the Zollverein in 1856, the mills were consuming 121,050 bales of American cotton and 64,900 bales of all other, which, in 1857, was increased to 158,650 and 77,300 bales respectively. The whole amount of cotton imported in 1855 was 118,820,546 pounds. In 1853, of 1,938,000 poods of raw cotton used in Russian factories, 1,814,282 poods were of American growth. In Austria, in 1856, there were 83,747,858 pounds introduced for consumption, the value of which was $10,938,634. The greater part is said to have come from the United States either by Bremen or Trieste. Of that introduced by Trieste, being in amount three eighths of the whole, one third was Egyptian. Of the 19,020,661 pounds of cotton imported into Sardinia in 1855, 11,621,797 pounds were from the United States, besides 4,059,785 from Great Britain, a part of which was also American. Into Antwerp, between January and October, 1857, 20,225,323 pounds were imported for consumption, of which 11,414,955 were from the United States, 5,305,573 pounds from England, and 3,333,585 pounds from the English East Indies. The import from the United States into Great Britain for 1856 is stated, on the authority of Sharp's Tables, at 780,040,016 pounds; from the East Indies at 180,496,624 pounds; and from all other countries than the United States, at 243,846,512. This leaves a balance in favor of the United States over all countries, in the consumption of England, of 536,193,504 pounds. (35 Cong. 1 Sess. Senate, Ex. Doc. No. 35, Mr. Claiborne's Report.)

From the above statement it may be clearly seen what would be the effect on the world at large if any serious interruption in the production of American cotton should occur.

www.ingramcontent.com/pod-product-compliance
Lightning Source LLC
La Vergne TN
LVHW050529100826
845148LV00002B/495

9781425520144